I0427697

 U.S. ENVIRONMENTAL PROTECTION AGENCY
OFFICE OF INSPECTOR GENERAL

## Audit Report

# Audit of EPA's Fiscal 2010 and 2009 Consolidated Financial Statements

Report No. 11-1-0015

November 15, 2010

## Abbreviations

| | |
|---|---|
| CFC | Cincinnati Finance Center |
| EPA | U.S. Environmental Protection Agency |
| FFMIA | Federal Financial Management Improvement Act of 1996 |
| FMFIA | Federal Managers' Financial Integrity Act of 1982 |
| GAO | U.S. Government Accountability Office |
| IFMS | Integrated Financial Management System |
| OIG | Office of Inspector General |
| OMB | Office of Management and Budget |
| RSSI | Required Supplementary Stewardship Information |
| SSC | Superfund State Contract |
| USAID | U.S. Agency for International Development |
| WCF | Working Capital Fund |

# At a Glance

*Catalyst for Improving the Environment*

## Why We Did This Audit

We performed this audit in accordance with the Government Management Reform Act, which requires the U.S. Environmental Protection Agency (EPA) to prepare, and the Office of Inspector General to audit, the Agency's financial statements each year. Our primary objectives were to determine whether:

- EPA's consolidated financial statements were fairly stated in all material respects.
- EPA's internal controls over financial reporting were in place.
- EPA management complied with applicable laws and regulations.

## Background

The requirement for audited financial statements was enacted to help bring about improvements in agencies' financial management practices, systems, and controls so that timely, reliable information is available for managing federal programs.

**For further information, contact our Office of Congressional, Public Affairs and Management at (202) 566-2391.**

**To view the full report, click on the following link:**
www.epa.gov/oig/reports/2011/20101115-11-1-0015.pdf

# Audit of EPA's Fiscal 2010 and 2009 Consolidated Financial Statements

## EPA Receives Unqualified Opinion

We rendered an unqualified opinion on EPA's Consolidated Financial Statements for fiscal 2010 and 2009, meaning that they were fairly presented and free of material misstatement.

## Internal Control Significant Deficiencies Noted

We noted the following four significant deficiencies:

- Further improvements are needed in reviewing the Superfund state contract unearned revenue spreadsheets.
- EPA should assess collectability of federal receivables and record allowances for doubtful accounts as needed.
- EPA needs to improve its controls for headquarters personal property.
- EPA needs to properly close the Fund Balance with Treasury when cancelling treasury symbols.

## Noncompliance With Laws and Regulations Noted

We noted one noncompliance issue involving EPA's need to continue efforts to reconcile intragovernmental transactions.

## Agency Comments and Office of Inspector General Evaluation

In a memorandum received on November 9, 2010, from the Chief Financial Officer, the Agency generally concurred with the issues raised and indicated it will take corrective actions. The Agency did not concur with two of our draft report recommendations. We have modified these recommendations to reflect information provided by the Chief Financial Officer in response to the draft report. The Agency's full response is included in Appendix II, and our analysis of the Agency's response is included in the body of the report.

**UNITED STATES ENVIRONMENTAL PROTECTION AGENCY**
WASHINGTON, D.C. 20460

November 15, 2010

## <u>MEMORANDUM</u>

**SUBJECT:**     Audit of EPA's Fiscal 2010 and 2009 Consolidated Financial Statements
Report No. 11-1-0015

**FROM:**     Arthur A. Elkins, Jr.
Inspector General

**TO:**     Barbara J. Bennett
Chief Financial Officer

Craig Hooks
Assistant Administrator for Administration and Resources Management

Attached is our report on the U.S. Environmental Protection Agency's (EPA's) fiscal 2010 and 2009 consolidated financial statements. We are reporting four significant deficiencies. We also identified an instance of noncompliance with laws and regulations related to reporting intragovernmental transactions. Attachment 3 contains the status of recommendations related to the material weaknesses, significant deficiencies, and noncompliances with laws and regulations reported in prior years' reports. The significant deficiencies and noncompliances included in Attachment 3 also apply for fiscal 2010.

The estimated cost of this report—calculated by multiplying the project's staff days by the applicable daily full cost billing rates in effect at the time—is $2,618,923.

This audit report represents the opinion of the Office of Inspector General, and the findings in this report do not necessarily represent the final EPA position. EPA managers, in accordance with established EPA audit resolution procedures, will make final determinations on the findings in this audit report. Accordingly, the findings described in this audit report are not binding upon EPA in any enforcement proceeding brought by EPA or the Department of Justice. We have no objections to the further release of this report to the public. This report will be available at http://www.epa.gov/oig.

In accordance with EPA Manual 2750, you are required to provide a written response to this report within 90 calendar days of the final report date. The response should address all issues and recommendations contained in Attachments 1 and 2. For corrective actions planned but not completed by the response date, reference to specific milestone dates will assist us in deciding whether or not to close this report in our audit tracking system. Your response will be posted on the OIG's public website, along with our memorandum commenting on your response. Your response should be provided as an Adobe PDF file that complies with the accessibility requirements of section 508 of the Rehabilitation Act of 1973, as amended. The final response should not contain data that you do not want to be released to the public; if your response contains such data, you should identify the data for redaction or removal.

Should you or your staff have any questions about the report, please contact Melissa Heist, Assistant Inspector General for Audit, at (202) 566-0899; or Paul Curtis, Director, Financial Statement Audits, at (202) 566-2523.

Attachments

cc: See Appendix III, Distribution

# Table of Contents

# Inspector General's Report on EPA's Fiscal 2010 and 2009 Consolidated Financial Statements

The Administrator
U.S. Environmental Protection Agency

We have audited the consolidated balance sheet of the U.S. Environmental Protection Agency (EPA) as of September 30, 2010 and 2009, and the related consolidated statements of net cost, net cost by goal, changes in net position, and custodial activity; and the combined statement of budgetary resources for the years then ended. These financial statements are the responsibility of EPA's management. Our responsibility is to express an opinion on these financial statements based upon our audit.

We conducted our audit in accordance with generally accepted government auditing standards; the standards applicable to financial statements contained in *Government Auditing Standards*, issued by the Comptroller General of the United States; and Office of Management and Budget (OMB) Bulletin 07-04, *Audit Requirements for Federal Financial Statements, as Amended September 23, 2009*. These standards require that we plan and perform the audit to obtain reasonable assurance about whether the financial statements are free of material misstatements. An audit includes examining, on a test basis, evidence supporting the amounts and disclosures in the financial statements. An audit also includes assessing the accounting principles used and significant estimates made by management, as well as evaluating the overall financial statement presentation. We believe that our audit provides a reasonable basis for our opinion.

The financial statements include expenses of grantees, contractors, and other federal agencies. Our audit work pertaining to these expenses included testing only within EPA. Audits of grants, contracts, and interagency agreements performed at a later date may disclose questioned costs of an amount undeterminable at this time. The U.S. Treasury collects and accounts for excise taxes that are deposited into the Superfund and Leaking Underground Storage Tank Trust Funds. The U.S. Treasury is also responsible for investing amounts not needed for current disbursements and transferring funds to EPA as authorized in legislation. Since the U.S. Treasury, and not EPA, is responsible for these activities, our audit work did not cover these activities.

The Office of Inspector General (OIG) is not independent with respect to amounts pertaining to OIG operations that are presented in the financial statements. The amounts included for the OIG are not material to EPA's financial statements. The OIG is organizationally independent with respect to all other aspects of the Agency's activities.

In our opinion, the consolidated financial statements present fairly, including the accompanying notes, in all material respects, the consolidated assets, liabilities, net position, net cost, net cost by goal, changes in net position, custodial activity, and combined budgetary resources of EPA as of and for the years ended September 30, 2010 and 2009, in conformity with accounting principles generally accepted in the United States of America.

## Review of EPA's Required Supplementary Stewardship Information, Required Supplementary Information, Supplemental Information, and Management's Discussion and Analysis

We obtained information from EPA management about its methods for preparing Required Supplementary Stewardship Information (RSSI), Required Supplementary Information, Supplemental Information, and Management's Discussion and Analysis, and reviewed this information for consistency with the financial statements. The Supplemental Information includes the unaudited Superfund Trust Fund financial statements for fiscal 2010 and 2009, which are being presented for additional analysis and are not a required part of the basic financial statements. However, our audit was not designed to express an opinion and, accordingly, we do not express an opinion on EPA's RSSI, Required Supplementary Information, Supplemental Information, and Management's Discussion and Analysis.

We did not identify any material inconsistencies between the information presented in EPA's consolidated financial statements and the information presented in EPA's RSSI, Required Supplementary Information, Supplemental Information, and Management's Discussion and Analysis.

## Evaluation of Internal Controls

As defined by OMB, internal control, as it relates to the financial statements, is a process, affected by the Agency's management and other personnel that is designed to provide reasonable assurance that the following objectives are met:

**Reliability of financial reporting**—Transactions are properly recorded, processed, and summarized to permit the preparation of the financial statements in accordance with generally accepted accounting principles, and assets are safeguarded against loss from unauthorized acquisition, use, or disposition.

**Compliance with applicable laws, regulations, and government-wide policies**— Transactions are executed in accordance with laws governing the use of budget authority, government-wide policies, laws identified by OMB, and other laws and regulations that could have a direct and material effect on the financial statements.

In planning and performing our audit, we considered EPA's internal controls over financial reporting by obtaining an understanding of the Agency's internal controls, determining whether internal controls had been placed in operation, assessing control risk, and performing tests of controls. We did this as a basis for designing our auditing procedures for the purpose of expressing an opinion on the financial statements and to comply with OMB audit guidance, not to express an opinion on internal control. Accordingly, we do not express an opinion on internal control over financial reporting nor on management's assertion on internal controls included in Management's Discussion and Analysis. We limited our internal control testing to those controls necessary to achieve the objectives described in OMB Bulletin No. 07-04, *Audit Requirements for Federal Financial Statements, as Amended September 23, 2009.* We did not test all internal controls relevant to operating objectives as broadly defined by the Federal Managers' Financial Integrity Act of 1982 (FMFIA), such as those controls relevant to ensuring efficient operations. Our consideration of the internal controls over financial reporting would not necessarily disclose all matters in the internal control over financial reporting that might be significant deficiencies. Under standards issued by the American Institute of Certified Public Accountants, a significant deficiency is a deficiency, or combination of deficiencies, that is less severe than a material weakness, yet important enough to merit attention by those charged with governance. A material weakness is a deficiency, or combination of deficiencies, such that there is a reasonable possibility that a material misstatement of the entity's financial statements will not be prevented, or detected and corrected on a timely basis. Because of inherent limitations in internal controls, misstatements, losses, or noncompliance may nevertheless occur and not be detected. We noted certain matters discussed below involving the internal control and its operation that we consider to be significant deficiencies, none of which are considered to be material weaknesses.

We noted four significant deficiencies, which are summarized below and detailed in Attachment 1.

### Further Improvements Needed in Reviewing the Superfund State Contract Unearned Revenue Spreadsheets

Although the Cincinnati Finance Center (CFC) worked with the regions in fiscal 2010 to improve the accuracy of the Superfund state contract (SSC) unearned revenue accrual, further improvements are needed. CFC and the regions did not thoroughly review the SSC spreadsheets and detect data errors that we found during our test work. The Chief Financial Officers Act requires that the integrated agency accounting and financial management system include complete and reliable information. By not performing a thorough review, EPA misstated the unearned revenue accrual in the fiscal 2010 financial statements.

### EPA Should Assess Collectability of Federal Receivables and Record Any Needed Allowances for Doubtful Accounts

EPA did not establish a federal allowance for doubtful accounts for receivables that were not billed timely and now may be uncollectible. Federal accounting standards require agencies to recognize receivables at their net realizable value. EPA considered federal debts to be fully collectible and did not have a policy to establish federal doubtful accounts until October 2010. By not timely reviewing debts, assessing the collectability of federal receivables, and establishing a federal allowance for doubtful accounts for uncollectible debt, EPA could be understating the uncollectible debt expense and overstating receivables in the financial statements.

### Improvements Needed in Controls for Headquarters Personal Property

EPA headquarters could not account for certain personal property items in fiscal 2010 as required by EPA's *Personal Property and Procedures Manual*. The primary cause is that headquarters mid-level management is not knowledgeable about Agency property management procedures. Because EPA could not account for these property items, it is not exercising proper control over $2.5 million of accountable personal property. As of May 28, 2010, EPA headquarters could not account for 2,272 accountable personal property items. Through subsequent searches, the number of missing items as of September 30, 2010, fell to 1,134. EPA headquarters determined that the acquisition cost of these missing items is $2,543,360. This is the second consecutive year we have reported this problem. In fiscal 2009, EPA headquarters did not inventory 1,804 items with an acquisition value of $6.3 million.

### EPA Improperly Closed Accounts When Cancelling Treasury Symbols

EPA did not properly close the Fund Balance with Treasury when cancelling treasury symbols on September 30, 2010. *Treasury Financial Manual Bulletin No. 2009-04* states that agencies must cancel any remaining balances (whether obligated or unobligated) in the account being cancelled. Valid receivables and payables associated with the cancelled Treasury Appropriation Fund Symbol still need to be included for financial reporting. EPA advanced funds to its Working Capital Fund (WCF) in fiscal 2002 and 2003. The WCF billed against those advances for all but $933,299. When the Treasury funds expired at the end of fiscal 2003, the WCF had not repaid the advance to the Environmental Program and Management Fund (treasury symbol 682/30108). The funds should have been repaid by the WCF when the funds originally expired. Subsequently, the treasury symbol 682/30108 became cancelled on September 30, 2010, and the advance still had not been repaid. EPA processed an entry to close out the treasury symbol, improperly expensing the advance as well as removing other liabilities. EPA stated that it followed its cancellation procedures and *Year End Closing Instructions.* The closing instructions state, "All open advances (GL 1400 account series) for appropriations being cancelled must be cleared by September 30." The instructions required EPA to remove any balance in an advance or liability account, and recognize expense and earned revenue in the current year. By doing so, EPA improperly eliminated advances and liabilities, and recognized current year expenditures and revenue.

Attachment 3 contains the status of issues reported in prior years' reports. The issues included in attachment 3 should be included in considering EPA's significant deficiencies for fiscal 2010. We reported less significant matters regarding internal controls in the form of position papers during the course of the audit. We will not issue a separate management letter.

### Comparison of EPA's FMFIA Report with Our Evaluation of Internal Controls

OMB Bulletin No. 07-04, *Audit Requirements for Federal Financial Statements, as Amended September 23, 2009*, requires us to compare material weaknesses disclosed during the audit with those material weaknesses reported in the Agency's FMFIA report that relate to the financial statements and identify material weaknesses disclosed by the audit that were not reported in the Agency's FMFIA report.

For financial statement audit and financial reporting purposes, OMB defines material weaknesses in internal control as a deficiency, or combination of deficiencies in internal control, such that there is a reasonable possibility that a material misstatement of the financial statements will not be prevented, or detected and corrected on a timely basis.

The Agency reported that no material weaknesses had been found in the design or operation of internal controls over financial reporting as of June 30, 2010. We did not identify any material weaknesses during the course of our audit. Details concerning our findings on significant deficiencies can be found in Attachment 1.

## Tests of Compliance With Laws and Regulations

EPA management is responsible for complying with laws and regulations applicable to the Agency. As part of obtaining reasonable assurance about whether the Agency's financial statements are free of material misstatement, we performed tests of its compliance with certain provisions of laws and regulations, noncompliance with which could have a direct and material effect on the determination of financial statement amounts, and certain other laws and regulations specified in OMB Bulletin No. 07-04, *Audit Requirements for Federal Financial Statements, as Amended September 23, 2009*. The OMB guidance requires that we evaluate compliance with federal financial management system requirements, including the requirements referred to in the Federal Financial Management Improvement Act of 1996 (FFMIA). We limited our tests of compliance to these provisions and did not test compliance with all laws and regulations applicable to EPA.

Providing an opinion on compliance with certain provisions of laws and regulations was not an objective of our audit and, accordingly, we do not express such an opinion. A number of ongoing investigations involving EPA's grantees and contractors could disclose violations of laws and regulations, but a determination about these cases has not been made.

### EPA Should Continue Efforts to Reconcile Intragovernmental Transactions

As of September 30, 2010, EPA reported $378 million in unreconciled differences with 48 trading partners for intragovernmental transactions. Of that amount, $271 million was reported by Treasury to be material differences. The remaining $107 million represents amounts reported for nonverifying agencies, accruals, timing differences, and other agencies whose differences were not reported as material. According to the *Treasury Financial Manual*, verifying agencies are those that are required to report in the Governmentwide Financial Report System. These include the 24 major Chief Financial Officers Act agencies and 11 other agencies material to the *Financial Report of the United States Government*. Any agency not required is a nonverifying agency. Treasury policy requires verifying agencies to confirm and reconcile intragovernmental transactions with their trading partners. Based on our review of correspondence with other agencies, EPA had difficulty reconciling these differences primarily because of differing accounting treatments and accrual methodologies among federal agencies, and because of a large reporting error made by one of EPA's trading partners. EPA's inability to reconcile its intragovernmental transactions contributes to a long-standing government-wide problem that hinders the ability of the U.S. Government Accountability Office to (GAO) render an opinion on the Consolidated Financial Statements of the Federal Government. Further details on this noncompliance issue are in Attachment 2.

### *Federal Financial Management Improvement Act Noncompliance*

Under FFMIA, we are required to report whether the Agency's financial management systems substantially comply with the federal financial management systems requirements, applicable federal accounting standards, and the United States Government Standard General Ledger at the transaction level. To meet the FFMIA requirement, we performed tests of compliance with FFMIA section 803(a) requirements and used the OMB guidance, *Memorandum M-09-06, Implementation Guidance for the Federal Financial Management Improvement Act dated January 9, 2009*, for determining substantial noncompliance with FFMIA. The results of our tests did not disclose any instances in which the Agency's financial management systems did not substantially comply with FFMIA requirements.

No other significant matters involving compliance with laws and regulations came to our attention during the course of the audit. We will not be issuing a separate management letter.

Our audit work was also performed to meet the requirements in Title 42, U.S. Code, section 9611(k), with respect to the Hazardous Substance Superfund Trust Fund, to conduct an annual audit of payments, obligations, reimbursements, or other uses of the fund. The material weaknesses and significant deficiencies reported above also relate to Superfund.

## Prior Audit Coverage

During previous financial or financial-related audits, we reported weaknesses that impacted our audit objectives in the following areas:

- Billing costs and reconciling unearned revenue for Superfund state contracts
- Misstated uncollectible debt
- Headquarters property items not inventoried
- Deobligating unneeded funds
- Integrated Financial Management System User Account Management
- Physical access controls at the Las Vegas Finance Center
- Security planning for Customer Technology Solutions equipment
- Reconciling and reporting intragovernmental transactions
- Financial database security oversight
- Assessing automated application processing controls for the Integrated Financial Management System

Attachment 3, Status of Prior Audit Report Recommendations, summarizes the current status of corrective actions taken on prior audit report recommendations related to these issues.

## Agency Comments and OIG Evaluation

In a memorandum dated November 9, 2010, the Office of the Chief Financial Officer responded to our draft report.

The rationale for our conclusions and a summary of the Agency comments are included in the appropriate sections of this report, and the Agency's complete response is included as Appendix II to this report.

This report is intended solely for the information and use of the management of EPA, OMB, and Congress, and is not intended to be and should not be used by anyone other than these specified parties.

Paul C. Curtis
Director, Financial Statement Audits
Office of Inspector General
U.S. Environmental Protection Agency
November 15, 2010

# Internal Control
# Significant Deficiencies

## Table of Contents

# 1 – Further Improvements Needed in Reviewing the Superfund State Contract Unearned Revenue Spreadsheets

Although CFC worked with the regions in fiscal 2010 to improve the accuracy of the SSC unearned revenue accrual, further improvements are needed. CFC and the regions did not thoroughly review the SSC spreadsheets and detect data errors that we found during our test work. The Chief Financial Officers Act requires that the integrated agency accounting and financial management system include complete and reliable information. By not performing a thorough review, EPA misstated the unearned revenue accrual in the fiscal 2010 financial statements.

CFC uses the SSC spreadsheets to calculate earned and unearned revenue for SSCs and to prepare quarterly accounting entries to adjust for quarterly activity. EPA overstated its fiscal 2010 fourth quarter SSC unearned revenue accrual by $3,630,833 and its unbilled costs by $858,100. We found errors in the fiscal 2010 third and fourth quarter SSC spreadsheet data, including errors in state cost estimates, state cost shares, credits, billings, and disbursements. We also identified several sites with questionable data that will require EPA's followup.

During our third quarter testing, we reviewed a sample of 20 SSC sites with unearned revenue of $13,546,608 from a universe of 480 sites totaling $45,061,760. We found 10 sites with errors that understated account 2312, Unearned Advances Non-Federal, by $375,338, and understated account 13PB, Unbilled SSC Work in Progress, by $410,498. By statistical projection of the errors, the most likely net overstatement or understatement of unearned revenue would be $5,650,742.

CFC corrected the 10 errors in the fourth quarter spreadsheet. The errors included:

- A site with SSC billings of $255,186 that were not entered on the SSC spreadsheet.
- Nine sites with incorrect disbursement amounts in the Hazardous Substance Superfund appropriation, fund code "T," entered on the spreadsheets that understated the spreadsheet disbursements by $4.6 million.

We also reviewed the data for all 480 sites on the spreadsheet for reasonableness. We identified 60 sites with (1) questionable data in credits, billings, or unearned revenue in excess of the state cost share; (2) no billings; and (3) no estimated site costs. Additionally, some of the 60 sites were closed sites with accrued unbilled costs. One site had a negative billing, and one site had negative credits and disbursements. The regions' responses to our questions indicated that the data for several sites were not current. For example, the regions did not always:

- Update the estimated site costs and state cost share for amended SSCs.
- Adjust the spreadsheet estimated costs and state cost share, credits, billings, and reimbursable disbursements for the effect of closed sites and refunds to the states.
- Use the correct transaction code for older refunds to properly reduce SSC billings.
- Transfer unused credits to other SSC sites when EPA completes the SSC work on a site.

From our analysis of the site data and the regions' responses, we identified 33 errors that overstated account 2312 by $5,166,394 and account 13PB by $1,753,032. CFC corrected 15 of the errors in the fourth quarter, leaving account 2312 overstated by $3,630,833 and account 13PB overstated by $858,100 at year-end. CFC stated that it will make the remaining corrections in the first quarter of fiscal 2011.

During fiscal 2010, CFC performed quarterly reviews of spreadsheet billings and disbursements to improve data accuracy. CFC also directed Superfund regional offices to verify that billings and disbursements in the spreadsheets were accurate and that closed sites were financially closed in the spreadsheets. However, CFC and the regions did not thoroughly review the SSC spreadsheet data to ensure that they were accurate prior to recording the accrual accounting entries in EPA's Integrated Financial Management System (IFMS). EPA should further improve the spreadsheet data accuracy.

FMFIA requires agencies to establish controls that reasonably assure that "revenues and expenditures applicable to agency operations are properly recorded and accounted for to permit the preparation of accounts and reliable financial and statistical reports." The Chief Financial Officers Act also requires the Agency to include financial reporting and internal controls that provide complete, reliable, consistent, and timely information in the integrated agency accounting and financial management system. EPA should have adequate internal controls to ensure that it properly records accruals for the SSC unearned revenue.

## Recommendations

We recommend that the Office of the Chief Financial Officer:

1. Work with the regions to review prior years' fund code "T" disbursements data on the SSC spreadsheets.

2. Work with the regions to review the spreadsheet data for the estimated site costs, state cost share, credits, and billings.

3. Require regions to report to CFC the SSC site closeout amounts, including the final actual site costs separated by "T" and "TR1" disbursements, final state share, and the amount of refund paid or final billing.

4. Review the quarterly SSC spreadsheets to determine whether the site data are reasonable and the resulting site calculations are logical. Specifically, review the data for billings, credits, or unearned revenue in excess of state cost shares; no estimated site costs; no billings; reimbursable "TR1" expenses in excess of billings; and closed sites with accrued unbilled costs or unearned revenue.

## Agency Comments and OIG Evaluation

The Agency concurred with our findings and recommendations.

## 2 – EPA Should Assess Collectability of Federal Receivables and Record Any Needed Allowances for Doubtful Accounts

EPA did not establish a federal allowance for doubtful accounts for receivables that were not billed timely and now may be uncollectible. Federal accounting standards require agencies to recognize receivables at their net realizable value. EPA considered federal debts to be fully collectible and until October 2010 did not have a policy to establish federal doubtful accounts. By not timely reviewing federal debts, assessing the collectability of federal receivables, and establishing a federal allowance for doubtful accounts for uncollectible debt, EPA could be understating the uncollectible debt expense and overstating receivables in the financial statements.

Historically, EPA did not establish allowances for delinquent federal debts because it considered all federal debts to be collectible. However, in October 2010, EPA issued a new policy to address delinquent federal receivables, Resources Management Directives System, 2540-12-P1, Intragovernmental Business Rules – Delinquent Federal Accounts Receivable. This policy states that CFC is responsible for managing federal receivables and exercising due diligence to collect amounts due to EPA from other federal agencies. Also, CFC is to conduct quarterly reviews of federal debt that is delinquent for a period of at least 3 years to determine whether to pursue collections efforts. The policy also states that if further collection efforts are not warranted, CFC should record an allowance for doubtful accounts in the accounting records. The debt is to be written off for those receivables deemed uncollectible.

As of September 2010, EPA's financial system had 45 open federal receivables totaling $22.8 million that were past their due date. Of this amount, $12.9 million represents 12 delinquent Superfund federal receivables established in February 1995 with the U.S. Department of Defense (Army) for the Twin City Army Ammunition Dump Site. Currently, EPA is working with OMB to obtain funding for the Twin Cities site for cleanup costs. The funding request of $6.3 million is 49 percent of the total receivables for Twin Cities. According to EPA, the Department of Defense included the entire $12.9 million in its books as a payable subsequent to September 30, 2010. As a result, EPA believes the entire receivable is now collectible. Because the receivable has been in doubt for so long and OMB has indicated that the funding request would be only $6.3 million, we believe EPA should establish an allowance for doubtful accounts for the remaining balance of the receivable and write off the negotiated amount when collected.

Of the remaining 33 delinquent federal receivables, totaling $9.8 million, we found that EPA did not timely bill or collect for 21 of the receivables totaling $9.5 million. EPA billed three federal agencies after those agencies had already deobligated the funds. One agency noted that EPA took more than 2 years after the performance period ended to submit a bill. We also identified nine other receivables totaling $8.7 million with which EPA had not taken adequate collection action. Another $7,000 was rejected by the billed agency because the interagency agreement was closed and the billing charges were over 9 years old. Other reasons cited as impacting collection efforts include other agencies' lack of congressional appropriation authority, waiting for additional funds to be included in other agencies' appropriations, and costs billed that exceeded the authorized amount on a Military Interdepartmental Purchase Request.

Statement of Federal Financial Accounting Standards Number 1 states that an allowance for estimated uncollectible amounts should be recognized to reduce the gross amount of receivables to its net realizable value. Loss estimation should be based on (a) the debtor's ability to pay, (b) the debtor's payment record and willingness to pay, and (c) the probable recovery of amounts from secondary sources.

In light of EPA's newly issued policy and the age of some outstanding federal receivables, we believe EPA should determine the collectability of all delinquent federal receivables and record any necessary accounting entries in the financial system to ensure that receivables are properly stated in the financial statements.

## Recommendations

We recommend that the Office of the Chief Financial Officer require the Office of Financial Services to:

5. Establish a federal allowance for $6.6 million, which remains on the Twin Cities site receivable, unless the Agency can obtain additional evidence from the Department of Defense that it intends to pay the debt.

6. Review collectability of open federal accounts receivables and establish an allowance and/or write-off.

7. Establish procedures to ensure that CFC timely bills federal agencies within their authorized appropriation period.

## Agency Comments and OIG Evaluation

The Agency considers the entire $12.9 million receivable from the Department of Defense collectible because the Department of Defense recorded a liability and has sought funding to partially pay the liability. However, negotiations with OMB and the Department of Defense have led to a funding request of only $6.3 million. Unless the Agency can provide additional evidence that the receivable is fully collectible, the Agency should establish an allowance for this receivable. The Agency concurred with our remaining findings and recommendations.

# 3 – Improvements Needed in Controls for Headquarters Personal Property

EPA headquarters could not account for some personal property items in fiscal 2010 as required by EPA's *Personal Property and Procedures Manual*. The primary cause was that headquarters mid-level management is not knowledgeable about Agency property management procedures. Because EPA could not account for these property items, it was not exercising proper control over $2.5 million of accountable personal property. As of May 28, 2010, EPA headquarters could not account for 2,272 accountable personal property items. Through subsequent searches, the number of missing items as of September 30, 2010, fell to 1,134. EPA headquarters determined that the acquisition cost of these missing items is $2,543,360. This is the second consecutive year we have reported this problem. In fiscal 2009, EPA headquarters did not inventory 1,804 items with an acquisition value of $6.3 million.

The Facilities Management Services Division is responsible for administering the EPA Personal Property Management Program. EPA defines accountable personal property "as non-expendable personal property with an acquisition cost of $5,000 or greater, EPA-leased personal property, or property identified as a sensitive item." EPA's *Personal Property and Procedures Manual*, section 3.1.1, states that each accountable area's personal property record must be maintained in IFMS, thus providing all needed data for effective personal property management (e.g., location, procurement, utilization, and disposal). The 1,134 missing items indicate that accurate personal property records are not being maintained. Inaccurate personal property records compromise EPA's property control system and can lead to the loss or misappropriation of Agency assets.

## Recommendations

We recommend that the Assistant Administrator for Administration and Resources Management require the Director, Facilities Management and Services Division, to:

8. Develop a management-level property management training course and require completion of the course by all EPA managers.

9. Adequately address and resolve the issue and determine why personal property items are missing.

## Agency Comments and OIG Evaluation

The Agency concurred with our findings and recommendations and offered additional information.

# 4 – EPA Improperly Closed Accounts
# When Cancelling Treasury Symbols

EPA did not properly close the Fund Balance with Treasury when cancelling treasury symbols on September 30, 2010. *Treasury Financial Manual Bulletin No. 2009-04* states that agencies must cancel any remaining balances (whether obligated or unobligated) in the account being cancelled. Valid receivables and payables associated with the cancelled Treasury Appropriation Fund Symbol still need to be included for financial reporting. EPA advanced funds to its WCF in fiscal 2002 and 2003. The WCF billed against those advances for all but $933,299. When the Treasury funds expired at the end of fiscal 2003, the WCF had not repaid the advance to the Environmental Program and Management Fund (treasury symbol 682/30108). The funds should have been repaid by WCF when the funds originally expired. Subsequently, the treasury symbol 682/30108 became cancelled on September 30, 2010, and the advance still had not been repaid. EPA processed an entry to close out the treasury symbol, improperly expensing the advance as well as removing other liabilities. EPA stated that it followed its Cancellation Procedures and *Year End Closing Instructions.* The closing instructions state, "All open advances (GL 1400 account series) for appropriations being cancelled must be cleared by September 30." The instructions required EPA to remove any balance in an advance or liability account, and recognize expense and earned revenue in the current year. By doing so, EPA improperly eliminated advances and liabilities, and recognized current year expenditures and revenue.

Treasury Financial Manual, Bulletin No. 2009-04 states:

> Agencies must close appropriation accounts available for obligation during a definite period after the account's obligation availability ends. Cancel any remaining balances (whether obligated or unobligated) in the account. These balances are unavailable for obligation or expenditure . . . Assets purchased by an [Agency] are not relieved from financial reporting simply because budget authority is cancelled. Also, agencies may have payables for which funding is cancelled, but the liability is still valid and the agency needs to report these payables for financial reporting.

EPA's WCF is a revolving fund authorized by law to finance a cycle of operations in which the costs for goods or services provided are charged to the users. The WCF operates like a commercial business within EPA; internal and external customers pay for services received, thereby generating revenue. WCF customers determine their WCF service requirements and provide advance funding to WCF, which is drawn down as WCF incurs costs for services provided.

EPA's cancellation procedures state:

> Once a seven-year period is lapsed, the fund is then cancelled. Cancelled funds can no longer disburse or collect money, nor can they adjust existing obligations (31 U.SC. 1552(a), 1555). All remaining funds must be returned to the Treasury general fund, and any subsequent collections should go to a general funds receipt account.

EPA did not properly close two cancelling treasury symbols at the end of fiscal 2010. EPA improperly eliminated advances to its WCF of $933,299, as well as other smaller advances and liabilities. EPA's WCF also improperly reduced its work-in-process account for the $933,299 and the liability for the advance. Our review of the WCF work-in-process account indicates that there were no unbilled amounts still outstanding from fiscal 2002/2003. EPA followed its incorrect cancellation procedures, which require eliminating the cancelled funds by closing out all payable (except expenditure transfers payable), liability, and all advance accounts to expense accounts, and closing out unearned advance account to earned revenue accounts. EPA's Year End Closing Instructions state, "All open advance (GL 1400 account series) for appropriations being cancelled must be cleared by September 30." By following the cancelling procedures, EPA improperly eliminated those balances and enabled the WCF to retain and possibly use funds for services that were never rendered and should be returned to Treasury.

The procedures that EPA used to remove the balances from the cancelled funds in the advance or liability account and to recognize them as an expense or revenue in the current year caused various general ledger accounts to be misstated. Consequently, the financial statements were misstated, although not materially as a whole.

## Recommendations

We recommend that the Office of the Chief Financial Officer:

10. Research and refund to Treasury cancelled funds as necessary.

11. Revise its cancellation procedures for the elimination of the balances from the cancelled treasury symbols.

12. Make appropriate adjustments to properly reflect balances.

## Agency Comments and OIG Evaluation

The Agency responded that it found that the $933,299 advance funds provided to the WCF for services were improperly reflected as drawn down from treasury symbol 683/40108 instead of 682/30108 and, therefore, does not believe the funds need to be returned to Treasury. The Agency recognized that an error occurred in reporting advance funds and it needs to make adjusting entries in fiscal 2011. The Agency was not able to fully support its claim in time for this report and, accordingly, we were not able to audit or determine the impact of the misposting on the treasury symbols involved. We revised our recommendation to suggest that the Agency research and refund cancelled funds as necessary. The Agency concurred with our remaining findings and recommendations.

# Compliance With Laws and Regulations

## Table of Contents

# 5 – EPA Should Continue Efforts to Reconcile Intragovernmental Transactions

As of September 30, 2010, EPA reported $378 million in unreconciled differences with 48 trading partners for intragovernmental transactions. Of that amount, $271 million was reported by Treasury to be material differences. The remaining $107 million represents amounts reported for nonverifying agencies, accruals, timing differences, and other agencies whose differences were not reported as material. According to the *Treasury Financial Manual*, verifying agencies are those that are required to report in the Governmentwide Financial Report System. These include the 24 major Chief Financial Officers Act agencies and 11 other agencies material to the *Financial Report of the United States Government*. Any agency not required is a nonverifying agency. Treasury policy requires verifying agencies to confirm and reconcile intragovernmental transactions with their trading partners. Based on our review of correspondence with other agencies, EPA had difficulty reconciling these differences primarily because of differing accounting treatments and accrual methodologies among federal agencies, and because of a large reporting error made by one of EPA's trading partners. EPA's inability to reconcile its intragovernmental transactions contributes to a long-standing government-wide problem that hinders the ability of GAO to render an opinion on the Consolidated Financial Statements of the Federal Government.

Treasury's fiscal 2010 fourth quarter Intragovernmental Activity Detail Report and Material Differences Report showed the following material differences for EPA:

| Federal agency | Difference | Category of difference |
|---|---|---|
| U.S. Department of the Treasury | $ 30,285,230 | Accounts Receivable/Payable |
| U.S. Department of Homeland Security | 33,343,985 | Buy/Sell Costs/Revenue |
| U.S. Agency for International Development | 207,659,275 | Buy/Sell Costs/Revenue |
| **Total** | **$ 271,288,490** | |

While the Agency has actively worked with its trading partners to reduce differences, differences continued to exist. The material differences reported with the U.S. Agency for International Development (USAID) were due to errors in reporting by USAID. USAID recognized the errors and stated that it would be making adjustments for these errors for the Government-wide Financial Report System closing package reporting. The difference with U.S. Department of Homeland Security stems mostly from activity related to timing differences in recording expenses related to working with the Coast Guard on the Gulf Oil spill. The Coast Guard has responded that it would adjust its expenses for the differences for the Government-wide Financial Report System closing package reporting. The remaining material difference with Treasury is due primarily to Treasury providing for an allowance on a $22 million judgment fund liability that EPA reports as the full amount, and $7.45 million for federal Superfund cost recovery settlements that Treasury will pay from the Judgment fund.

During fiscal 2010, EPA made significant efforts to reconcile its intragovernmental activity on a quarterly basis with its partners and has been able to identify the causes of material differences and work with other agencies to resolve them. However, unreconciled differences persist. According to GAO's *Auditor's Report on the Fiscal Year 2009 Financial Report of the U.S. Government,* the federal government's inability to adequately account for and reconcile intragovernmental activity and balances between federal entities is a major impediment preventing GAO from rendering an opinion on the accrual-based consolidated financial statements of the federal government.

## Recommendation

We recommend that the Office of the Chief Financial Officer:

13. Continue efforts to reconcile EPA's intragovernmental transactions and make appropriate adjustments to comply with federal financial reporting requirements.

## Agency Comments and OIG Evaluation

The Agency concurred with our findings and recommendation.

# Status of Prior Audit Report Recommendations

EPA is continuing to strengthen its audit management to address audit followup issues and complete corrective actions expeditiously and effectively to improve environmental results. The Chief Financial Officer is the Agency followup official and is responsible for ensuring that corrective actions are implemented. During fiscal 2010, the Office of the Chief Financial Officer continued to conduct the onsite reviews of national and program offices, which it initiated in fiscal 2009. The reviews focus on offices' audit followup procedures and their use of the Management Audit Tracking System, or MATS. The reviews are designed to promote sound audit management; increase Agency awareness of, accountability for, and completion of unimplemented corrective actions; and ensure that audit followup data are accurate and complete. The Office of the Chief Financial Officer completed seven of these on-site reviews in fiscal 2010, including three regional offices and four national program offices. These reviews will be performed on an ongoing, rotating basis.

The Agency has continued to make progress in completing corrective actions from prior years. The status of issues from prior financial statement audits and other audits with findings and recommendations that could have a material effect on financial statements and have corrective actions in process are listed in the following tables.

| Significant deficiencies – Corrective actions in process |
|---|
| • **Automated Application Processing Controls for IFMS**<br>EPA has taken additional steps to correct this open issue by undertaking a project to replace its core financial application. The new EPA Financial System is anticipated to "go live" in October 2012. We will continue to report a reportable condition concerning our inability to test application controls due to insufficient system documentation until the new system is implemented. |
| • **EPA Needs to Strengthen Financial Database Security Oversight and Monitor Compliance (Report No. 2007-P-00017)**<br>EPA did not complete all corrective actions related to reviewing the effectiveness of its followup procedures and update the procedures accordingly. The critical patch reports being shared and monitored as a part of the process did not include all operating systems and databases used by the Agency. EPA also has neither implemented procedures to escalate critical patch issues to appropriate management for resolution nor agreed to a course of action for when offices must mitigate the identified vulnerability. EPA indicated that it plans to complete these remaining corrective actions by July 2011. |
| • **EPA Needs to Improve Billing and Reconciling of Costs Under Superfund State Contracts**<br>During fiscal 2010, the Agency took corrective actions to reconcile SSC funds and credits in the general ledger to subsidiary accounts. EPA's corrective actions reduced the significance of the SSC internal control weakness from a material weakness to a significant deficiency. As described in Attachment 1, Significant Deficiencies, further improvements are needed in reviewing the SSC unearned revenue accrual spreadsheets. EPA still needs to work with regions to review spreadsheet data for prior years' fund code "T" disbursements, estimated site costs, state cost share, credits, and billings. EPA also needs to review the quarterly SSC accrual spreadsheet site data for reasonableness and require regions to report to the CFC the SSC site closeout amounts. |

| Significant deficiencies – Corrective actions in process |
|---|
| • **EPA Misstated Uncollectible Debt and Other Related Accounts**<br>In fiscal 2009, we recommended that EPA review and update the accounting model for fiscal 2010. In response to our recommendation, EPA noted that it would review the impact of accounting entries, including standard vouchers for billing documents, provide account models as needed, and provide technical advice as appropriate. EPA did not change the model in 2010, which resulted in an improper credit balance in the uncollectible debt expense account. EPA should address the causes for the credit balance in the uncollectible debt expense account and update the accounting model. |
| • **Headquarters Property Items Not Inventoried**<br>The Agency has not taken sufficient action to address the weakness we noted in the headquarters annual personal property inventory. As described in Attachment 1, Significant Deficiencies, EPA headquarters could not account for 1,134 personal property items in fiscal 2010. |
| • **Unneeded Funds Not Deobligated Timely**<br>While the Agency made significant efforts to complete two corrective actions to address last year's finding recommendation, it did not finish implementing the actions. Specifically, the Agency has not implemented training to ensure the effectiveness of its new policy on unliquidated obligations. We identified $1.4 million in inactive funds that are no longer needed and can be deobligated. |
| • **Integrated Financial Management System User Account Management Needs Improvement**<br>EPA is making progress on completing the agreed-upon corrective actions. To date, EPA has updated its processes to require the security administrator to work with requesting officials to ensure users are given the appropriate system access. EPA also implemented detective controls to correct instances in which access rights did not match rights requested and to check the system for terminated personnel. EPA submitted a *Separation of Duties Policy and Procedure* for formal Agency approval. The recommendations associated with the implementation of these documents should remain open until they are implemented. EPA plans to complete actions to remove access rights for personnel with incompatible duties and implement a system control to prevent assignment of incompatible duties by December 30, 2010. EPA has not established milestone dates for when it will implement a policy to notify financial systems owners of transferred/terminated personnel or review reports of terminated employees to remove them from the finance systems due to potential changes needed in the Human Resources System that may affect this process. |
| • **EPA Needs to Improve Physical Security at Its Offices in Las Vegas, Nevada (Report No. 10-P-0059)**<br>The Agency indicated that it is in the process of implementing the agreed-upon corrective actions associated with the recommendations in this report. The Agency's corrective action plan indicates that the final corrective action associated with this report will be completed by September 30, 2011. As a part of the agreed-upon corrective action plan, after all of the other corrective actions have been completed, EPA will conduct an assessment to ensure that the procedures are implemented and working as management intends by September 30, 2011. |
| • **Improved Security Planning Needed for the Customer Technology Solutions Project (Report No. 10-P-0028)**<br>EPA indicated that it had not yet completed the corrective actions associated with this audit and is in the process of updating the associated corrective action plan. EPA has not provided a milestone date for when it plans to complete the corrective actions associated with this report's recommendations. |

Source:  OIG analysis.


| Compliance with laws and regulations – Corrective actions in process |
|---|
| • **EPA needs to improve reconciliation of differences with trading partners**<br>The Agency has actively worked with its trading partners to reduce unreconciled differences. However, as described in Attachment 2, EPA reported $378 million in unreconciled differences for intragovernmental transactions with 48 trading partners. |

Source:  OIG analysis.

# Status of Current Recommendations and Potential Monetary Benefits

| | | RECOMMENDATIONS | | | | POTENTIAL MONETARY BENEFITS (in $000s) | |
|---|---|---|---|---|---|---|---|
| Rec. No. | Page No. | Subject | Status[1] | Action Official | Planned Completion Date | Claimed Amount | Agreed To Amount |
| 1 | 10 | Work with the regions to review prior years' fund code "T" disbursements data on the SSC spreadsheets. | | Office of the Chief Financial Officer | | | |
| 2 | 10 | Work with the regions to review the spreadsheet data for the estimated site costs, state cost share, credits, and billings. | | Office of the Chief Financial Officer | | | |
| 3 | 10 | Require regions to report to CFC the SSC site closeout amounts, including the final actual site costs separated by "T" and "TR1" disbursements, final state share, and the amount of refund paid or final billing. | | Office of the Chief Financial Officer | | | |
| 4 | 10 | Review the quarterly SSC spreadsheets to determine whether the site data are reasonable and the resulting site calculations are logical. Specifically, review the data for billings, credits, or unearned revenue in excess of state cost shares; no estimated site costs; no billings; reimbursable "TR1" expenses in excess of billings; and closed sites with accrued unbilled costs or unearned revenue. | | Office of the Chief Financial Officer | | | |
| 5 | 12 | Require the Office of Financial Services to establish a federal allowance for $6.6 million, which remains on the Twin Cities site receivable, unless the Agency can obtain additional evidence from the Department of Defense that it intends to pay the debt. | | Office of the Chief Financial Officer | | | |
| 6 | 12 | Require the Office of Financial Services to review collectability of open federal accounts receivables and establish an allowance and/or write-off. | | Office of the Chief Financial Officer | | | |
| 7 | 12 | Require the Office of Financial Services to establish procedures to ensure that CFC timely bills federal agencies within their authorized appropriation period. | | Office of the Chief Financial Officer | | | |
| 8 | 13 | Require the Director, Facilities Management and Services Division, to develop a management-level property management training course and require completion of the course by all EPA managers. | | Assistant Administrator for Administration and Resources Management | | | |
| 9 | 13 | Require the Director, Facilities Management and Services Division, to adequately address and resolve the issue and determine why personal property items are missing. | | Assistant Administrator for Administration and Resources Management | | | |
| 10 | 15 | Research and refund to Treasury cancelled funds as necessary. | | Office of the Chief Financial Officer | | | |

## RECOMMENDATIONS

| Rec. No. | Page No. | Subject | Status[1] | Action Official | Planned Completion Date | Claimed Amount | Agreed To Amount |
|---|---|---|---|---|---|---|---|
| 11 | 15 | Revise its cancellation procedures for the elimination of the balances from the cancelled treasury symbols. | | Office of the Chief Financial Officer | | | |
| 12 | 15 | Make appropriate adjustments to properly reflect balances. | | Office of the Chief Financial Officer | | | |
| 13 | 18 | Continue efforts to reconcile EPA's intragovernmental transactions and make appropriate adjustments to comply with federal financial reporting requirements. | | Office of the Chief Financial Officer | | | |
| | | **Note:** We identified $1.4 million in inactive funds that are no longer needed and can be deobligated. | | | | $1,400.0 | |

[1] O = recommendation is open with agreed-to corrective actions pending
C = recommendation is closed with all agreed-to actions completed
U = recommendation is undecided with resolution efforts in progress

# EPA's Fiscal 2010 and 2009 Consolidated Financial Statements

## SECTION II
## FINANCIAL SECTION

# Principal Financial Statements

## Financial Statements

1. Consolidated Balance Sheet
2. Consolidated Statement of Net Cost
3. Consolidated Statement of Net Cost by Goal
4. Consolidating Statement of Changes in Net Position
5. Combined Statement of Budgetary Resources
6. Statement of Custodial Activity

## Notes to Financial Statements

| | |
|---|---|
| Note 1. | Summary of Significant Accounting Policies |
| Note 2. | Fund Balance with Treasury (FBWT) |
| Note 3. | Cash and Other Monetary Assets |
| Note 4. | Investments |
| Note 5. | Accounts Receivable, Net |
| Note 6. | Other Assets |
| Note 7. | Loans Receivable, Net |
| Note 8. | Accounts Payable and Accrued Liabilities |
| Note 9. | General Property, Plant and Equipment (PP& E) |
| Note 10. | Debt Due to Treasury |
| Note 11. | Stewardship Land |
| Note 12. | Custodial Liability |
| Note 13. | Other Liabilities |
| Note 14. | Leases |
| Note 15. | FECA Actuarial Liabilities |
| Note 16. | Cashout Advances, Superfund |
| Note 17. | Unexpended Appropriations – Other Funds |
| Note 18. | Commitments and Contingencies |
| Note 19. | Earmarked Funds |
| Note 20. | Exchange Revenues, Statement of Net Cost |
| Note 21. | Intragovernmental Costs and Exchange Revenue |
| Note 22. | Cost of Stewardship Land |
| Note 23 | Environmental Cleanup Costs |
| Note 24. | State Credits |
| Note 25. | Preauthorized Mixed Funding Agreements |
| Note 26. | Custodial Revenues and Accounts Receivable |
| Note 27. | Reconciliation of President's Budget to Statement of Budgetary Resources |

## Notes to Financial Statements (continued)

Note 28.  Recoveries and Resources Not Available, Statement of Budgetary Resources
Note 29.  Unobligated Balances Available
Note 30.  Undelivered Orders at the End of the Period
Note 31.  Offsetting Receipts
Note 32.  Transfers-In and Out, Statement of Changes in Net Position
Note 33.  Imputed Financing
Note 34.  Payroll and Benefits Payable
Note 35.  Other Adjustments, Statement of Changes in Net Position
Note 36.  Non-exchange Revenue, Statement of Changes in Net Position
Note 37.  Reconciliation of Net Cost of Operations to Budget
Note 38.  Amounts Held By Treasury (Unaudited)
Note 39.  2004 Antideficiency Act Violation Reported in 2010

## Required Supplementary Information (Unaudited)

1.  Deferred Maintenance
2.  Stewardship Land
3.  Supplemental Statement of Budgetary Resources

## Required Supplementary Stewardship Information (Unaudited)

## Supplemental Information and Other Reporting Requirements (Unaudited)

Superfund Financial Statements and Related Notes

# Environmental Protection Agency
## Consolidated Balance Sheets
## As of September 30, 2010 and 2009
## (Dollars in Thousands)

| | | FY 2010 | | FY 2009 |
|---|---|---|---|---|
| **ASSETS** | | | | |
| Intragovernmental: | | | | |
| Fund Balance With Treasury (Note 2) | $ | 14,603,024 | $ | 15,557,917 |
| Investments (Note 4) | | 7,243,613 | | 6,879,948 |
| Accounts Receivable, Net (Note 5) | | 45,698 | | 39,362 |
| Other (Note 6) | | 223,296 | | 214,831 |
| Total Intragovernmental | $ | 22,115,631 | $ | 22,692,058 |
| | | | | |
| Cash and Other Monetary Assets (Note 3) | | 10 | | 10 |
| Accounts Receivable, Net (Note 5) | | 417,535 | | 817,844 |
| Loans Receivable, Net - Non-Federal (Note 7) | | 5,254 | | 11,645 |
| Property, Plant & Equipment, Net (Note 9) | | 915,121 | | 852,488 |
| Other (Note 6) | | 2,834 | | 2,228 |
| **Total Assets** | $ | **23,456,385** | $ | **24,376,273** |
| | | | | |
| Stewardship PP& E (Note 11 ) | | | | |
| | | | | |
| **LIABILITIES** | | | | |
| Intragovernmental: | | | | |
| Accounts Payable and Accrued Liabilities (Note 8) | | 51,325 | | 76,054 |
| Debt Due to Treasury (Note 10) | | 4,844 | | 9,983 |
| Custodial Liability (Note 12) | | 52,751 | | 71,200 |
| Other (Note 13) | | 132,286 | | 140,645 |
| Total Intragovernmental | $ | 241,206 | $ | 297,882 |
| | | | | |
| Accounts Payable & Accrued Liabilities (Note 8) | $ | 1,031,448 | $ | 865,764 |
| Pensions & Other Actuarial Liabilities (Note 15) | | 44,938 | | 44,122 |
| Environmental Cleanup Costs (Note 23) | | 20,154 | | 19,494 |
| Cashout Advances, Superfund (Note 16) | | 636,673 | | 572,412 |
| Commitments & Contingencies (Note 18) | | 4,373 | | 4,573 |
| Payroll & Benefits Payable (Note 34) | | 264,975 | | 250,617 |
| Other (Note 13) | | 99,996 | | 115,918 |
| Total Liabilities | $ | 2,343,763 | $ | 2,170,782 |
| | | | | |
| **NET POSITION** | | | | |
| Unexpended Appropriations - Other Funds (Note 17) | | 13,342,784 | | 14,536,347 |
| Cumulative Results of Operations - Earmarked Funds (Note 19) | | 7,152,382 | | 7,086,476 |
| Cumulative Results of Operations - Other Funds | | 617,456 | | 582,668 |
| | | | | |
| Total Net Position | | 21,112,622 | | 22,205,491 |
| | | | | |
| **Total Liabilities and Net Position** | $ | **23,456,385** | $ | **24,376,273** |

**The accompanying notes are an integral part of these financial statements.**

# Environmental Protection Agency
## Consolidated Statements of Net Cost
## For the Periods Ending September 30, 2010 and 2009
## (Dollars in Thousands)

|  | FY 2010 | FY 2009 |
|---|---|---|
| **COSTS** |  |  |
| Gross Costs (Note 21) | $ 12,406,265 | $ 8,920,963 |
| Less: |  |  |
| Earned Revenue (Notes 20, 21) | 693,484 | 773,612 |
| **NET COST OF OPERATIONS (Note 21)** | $ 11,712,781 | $ 8,147,351 |

**The accompanying notes are an integral part of these financial statements.**

# Environmental Protection Agency
## Consolidated Statements of Net Cost by Goal
## For the Period Ending September 30, 2010
## (Dollars in Thousands)

| | Clean Air | Clean & Safe Water | Land Preservation & Restoration | Healthy Communities & Ecosystems | Compliance & Environmental Stewardship |
|---|---|---|---|---|---|
| **Costs:** | | | | | |
| Intragovernmental | $ 170,677 | $ 193,456 | $ 342,734 | $ 293,850 | $ 182,299 |
| With the Public | 1,048,124 | 6,197,330 | 2,096,211 | 1,265,653 | 615,931 |
| Total Costs (Note 21) | 1,218,801 | 6,390,786 | 2,438,945 | 1,559,503 | 798,230 |
| | | | | | |
| Less: | | | | | |
| Earned Revenue, Federal | 18,923 | 2,803 | 103,687 | 64,034 | 3,400 |
| Earned Revenue, non Federal | 5,906 | 2,524 | 446,569 | 44,144 | 1,494 |
| Total Earned Revenue (Notes 20,21) | 24,829 | 5,327 | 550,256 | 108,178 | 4,894 |
| | | | | | |
| **NET COST OF OPERATIONS (Note 21)** | $ 1,193,972 | $ 6,385,459 | $ 1,888,689 | $ 1,451,325 | $ 793,336 |

| | Consolidated Totals |
|---|---|
| **Costs:** | |
| Intragovernmental | $ 1,183,016 |
| With the Public | $ 11,223,249 |
| Total Costs (Note 21) | 12,406,265 |
| | |
| Less: | |
| Earned Revenue, Federal | $ 192,847 |
| Earned Revenue, non Federal | $ 500,637 |
| Total Earned Revenue (Notes 20,21) | 693,484 |
| | |
| **NET COST OF OPERATIONS (Note 21)** | $ 11,712,781 |

**The accompanying notes are an integral part of these financial statements.**

# Environmental Protection Agency
## Consolidated Statements of Net Cost by Goal
## For the Period Ending September 30, 2009
## (Dollars in Thousands)

| | Clean Air | Clean & Safe Water | Land Preservation & Restoration | Healthy Communities & Ecosystems | Compliance & Environmental Stewardship |
|---|---|---|---|---|---|
| **Costs:** | | | | | |
| Intragovernmental | $ 187,484 | $ 191,558 | $ 386,549 | $ 271,028 | $ 207,660 |
| With the Public | 874,787 | 3,236,903 | 1,821,301 | 1,134,155 | 609,538 |
| Total Costs (Note 21) | 1,062,271 | 3,428,461 | 2,207,850 | 1,405,183 | 817,198 |
| **Less:** | | | | | |
| Earned Revenue, Federal | 15,455 | 4,758 | 101,767 | 20,047 | 4,071 |
| Earned Revenue, non Federal | 3,036 | 3,208 | 580,119 | 42,267 | (1,116) |
| Total Earned Revenue (Notes 20, 21) | 18,491 | 7,966 | 681,886 | 62,314 | 2,955 |
| **NET COST OF OPERATIONS (Note 21)** | $ 1,043,780 | $ 3,420,495 | $ 1,525,964 | $ 1,342,869 | $ 814,243 |

| | Consolidated Totals |
|---|---|
| **Costs:** | |
| Intragovernmental | $ 1,244,279 |
| With the Public | $ 7,676,684 |
| Total Costs | 8,920,963 |
| **Less:** | |
| Earned Revenue, Federal | $ 146,098 |
| Earned Revenue, non Federal | $ 627,514 |
| Total Earned Revenue (Notes 20, 21) | 773,612 |
| **NET COST OF OPERATIONS (Note 21)** | $ 8,147,351 |

**The accompanying notes are an integral part of these financial statements.**

# Environmental Protection Agency
## Consolidating Statements of Changes in Net Position
## For the Period Ending September 30, 2010
## (Dollars in Thousands)

|  |  | FY 2010 Earmarked Funds |  | FY 2010 All Other Funds |  | FY 2010 Consolidated Total |
|---|---|---|---|---|---|---|
| **Cumulative Results of Operations:** |  |  |  |  |  |  |
| **Net Position - Beginning of Period** |  | 7,086,476 |  | 582,668 |  | 7,669,144 |
| Beginning Balances, as Adjusted | $ | 7,086,476 | $ | 582,668 | $ | 7,669,144 |
| **Budgetary Financing Sources:** |  |  |  |  |  |  |
| Appropriations Used |  | - |  | 11,294,823 |  | 11,294,823 |
| Nonexchange Revenue - Securities Investment (Note 36) |  | 130,504 |  | - |  | 130,504 |
| Nonexchange Revenue - Other (Note 36) |  | 213,984 |  | - |  | 213,984 |
| Transfers In/Out (Note 32) |  | (20,789) |  | 33,859 |  | 13,070 |
| Trust Fund Appropriations |  | 1,280,570 |  | (1,280,570) |  | - |
| Total Budgetary Financing Sources | $ | 1,604,269 | $ | 10,048,112 | $ | 11,652,381 |
| **Other Financing Sources (Non-Exchange)** |  |  |  |  |  |  |
| Transfers In/Out (Note 32) |  | - |  | (546) |  | (546) |
| Imputed Financing Sources (Note 33) |  | 27,022 |  | 134,618 |  | 161,640 |
| Total Other Financing Sources | $ | 27,022 | $ | 134,072 | $ | 161,094 |
| Net Cost of Operations |  | (1,565,385) |  | (10,147,396) |  | (11,712,781) |
| Net Change |  | 65,906 |  | 34,788 |  | 100,694 |
| **Cumulative Results of Operations** | $ | **7,152,382** | $ | **617,456** | $ | **7,769,838** |

|  |  | FY 2010 Earmarked Funds |  | FY 2010 All Other Funds |  | FY 2010 Consolidated Total |
|---|---|---|---|---|---|---|
| **Unexpended Appropriations:** |  |  |  |  |  |  |
| **Net Position - Beginning of Period** |  | - |  | 14,536,347 |  | 14,536,347 |
| Beginning Balances, as Adjusted |  | - |  | 14,536,347 |  | 14,536,347 |
| **Budgetary Financing Sources:** |  |  |  |  |  |  |
| Appropriations Received |  | - |  | 10,182,421 |  | 10,182,421 |
| Appropriations Transferred In/Out (Note 32) |  | - |  | (17,000) |  | (17,000) |
| Other Adjustments (Note 35) |  | - |  | (65,989) |  | (65,989) |
| Appropriations Used |  | - |  | (11,292,995) |  | (11,292,995) |
| Total Budgetary Financing Sources |  | - |  | (1,193,563) |  | (1,193,563) |
| **Total Unexpended Appropriations** |  | - |  | 13,342,784 |  | 13,342,784 |
| **TOTAL NET POSITION** | $ | **7,152,382** | $ | **13,960,240** | $ | **21,112,622** |

**The accompanying notes are an integral part of these financial statements.**

# Environmental Protection Agency
## Consolidating Statements of Changes in Net Position
## For the Periods Ending September 30, 2009
### (Dollars in Thousands)

| | | FY 2009 Earmarked Funds | | FY 2009 All Other Funds | | FY 2009 Consolidated Total |
|---|---|---|---|---|---|---|
| **Cumulative Results of Operations:** | | | | | | |
| | | | | | | |
| **Net Position - Beginning of Period** | | 6,160,531 | | 555,766 | | 6,716,297 |
| Beginning Balances, as Adjusted | $ | 6,160,531 | $ | 555,766 | $ | 6,716,297 |
| | | | | | | |
| **Budgetary Financing Sources:** | | | | | | |
| Appropriations Used | | - | | 8,504,157 | | 8,504,157 |
| Nonexchange Revenue - Securities Investment (Note 36) | | 176,168 | | - | | 176,168 |
| Nonexchange Revenue - Other (Note 36) | | 188,245 | | - | | 188,245 |
| Transfers In/Out (Note 32) | | (39,705) | | 57,392 | | 17,687 |
| Trust Fund Appropriations | | 1,747,911 | | (1,747,911) | | - |
| Total Budgetary Financing Sources | $ | 2,072,619 | $ | 6,813,638 | $ | 8,886,257 |
| | | | | | | |
| **Other Financing Sources (Non-Exchange)** | | | | | | |
| Transfers In/Out (Note 32) | | (84) | | 694 | | 610 |
| Imputed Financing Sources (Note 33) | | 28,975 | | 184,356 | | 213,331 |
| Total Other Financing Sources | $ | 28,891 | $ | 185,050 | $ | 213,941 |
| | | | | | | |
| Net Cost of Operations | | (1,175,565) | | (6,971,786) | | (8,147,351) |
| | | | | | | |
| Net Change | | 925,945 | | 26,902 | | 952,847 |
| | | | | | | |
| **Cumulative Results of Operations** | $ | **7,086,476** | $ | **582,668** | $ | **7,669,144** |
| | | | | | | |
| | | | | | | |
| **Unexpended Appropriations:** | | | | | | |
| | | | | | | |
| **Net Position - Beginning of Period** | | - | | 8,674,710 | | 8,674,710 |
| Beginning Balances, as Adjusted | $ | - | $ | 8,674,710 | $ | 8,674,710 |
| | | | | | | |
| **Budgetary Financing Sources:** | | | | | | |
| Appropriations Received | | | | 14,406,298 | | 14,406,298 |
| Appropriations Transferred In/Out (Note 32) | | | | (10,953) | | (10,953) |
| Other Adjustments (Note 35) | | | | (29,551) | | (29,551) |
| Appropriations Used | | | | (8,504,157) | | (8,504,157) |
| Total Budgetary Financing Sources | | - | | 5,861,637 | | 5,861,637 |
| | | | | | | |
| **Total Unexpended Appropriations** | | - | | 14,536,347 | | 14,536,347 |
| | | | | | | |
| **TOTAL NET POSITION** | $ | **7,086,476** | $ | **15,119,015** | $ | **22,205,491** |

**The accompanying notes are an integral part of these financial statements.**

# Environmental Protection Agency
## Combined Statements of Budgetary Resources
### For the Periods Ending September 30, 2010 and 2009
### (Dollars in Thousands)

| | FY 2010 | | FY 2009 |
|---|---:|---|---:|
| **BUDGETARY RESOURCES** | | | |
| Unobligated Balance, Brought Forward, October 1: | $ 3,703,022 | $ | 3,551,880 |
| Adjusted Subtotal | 3,703,022 | | 3,551,880 |
| Recoveries of Prior Year Unpaid Obligations (Note 28) | 277,771 | | 220,329 |
| Budgetary Authority: | | | |
| Appropriation | 10,256,166 | | 15,276,374 |
| Borrowing Authority | 52 | | 5 |
| Spending Authority from Offsetting Collections | | | |
| Earned: | | | |
| Collected | 918,786 | | 631,378 |
| Change in Receivables from Federal Sources | (1,746) | | 2,884 |
| Change in Unfilled Customer Orders: | | | |
| Advance Received | 234,559 | | 29,183 |
| Without Advance from Federal Sources | (132,489) | | (93,701) |
| Anticipated for Rest of Year, Without Advances | 0 | | - |
| Previously Unavailable | - | | - |
| Expenditure Transfers from Trust Funds | 36,809 | | 57,392 |
| Total Spending Authority from Offsetting Collections | 1,055,919 | | 627,136 |
| Nonexpenditure Transfers, Net, Anticipated and Actual (Note 32) | 1,369,345 | | 1,371,077 |
| Temporarily Not Available Pursuant to Public Law (Note 28) | (11,800) | | - |
| Permanently Not Available (Note 28) | (73,453) | | (32,732) |
| **Total Budgetary Resources (Note 27)** | $ 16,577,022 | $ | 21,014,069 |
| | | | |
| **STATUS OF BUDGETARY RESOURCES** | | | |
| Obligations Incurred: | | | |
| Direct | $ 11,260,452 | $ | 16,740,272 |
| Reimbursable | 690,229 | | 570,775 |
| Total Obligations Incurred (Note 27) | 11,950,681 | | 17,311,047 |
| Unobligated Balances: | | | |
| Apportioned (Note 29) | 4,430,813 | | 3,440,829 |
| Exempt from Apportionment | - | | - |
| Total Unobligated Balances | 4,430,813 | | 3,440,829 |
| Unobligated Balances Not Available (Note 29) | 195,528 | | 262,193 |
| **Total Status of Budgetary Resources** | $ 16,577,022 | $ | 21,014,069 |

**The accompanying notes are an integral part of these financial statements.**

# Environmental Protection Agency
## Combined Statements of Budgetary Resources
### For the Periods Ending September 30, 2010 and 2009
### (Dollars in Thousands)

|  | | FY 2010 | | FY 2009 |
|---|---|---|---|---|
| **CHANGE IN OBLIGATED BALANCE** | | | | |
| Obligated Balance, Net: | | | | |
|    Unpaid Obligations, Brought Forward, October 1 | $ | 15,788,389 | $ | 9,368,094 |
|      Adjusted Total | | 15,788,389 | | 9,368,094 |
|    Less: Uncollected Customer Payments from Federal Sources, | | | | |
|    Brought Forward, October 1 | | (573,824) | | (666,246) |
|      Total Unpaid Obligated Balance, Net | | 15,214,565 | | 8,701,848 |
| Obligations Incurred, Net (Note 27) | | 11,950,681 | | 17,311,047 |
| Less: Gross Outlays (Note 27) | | (13,588,391) | | (10,670,422) |
| Obligated Balance Transferred, Net: | | | | |
|    Actual Transfers, Unpaid Obligations | | - | | - |
|    Actual Transfers, Uncollected Customer Payments from Federal | | - | | - |
|      Total Unpaid Obligated Balance Transferred, Net | | - | | - |
| Less: Recoveries of Prior Year Unpaid Obligations, Actual (Note 28) | | (277,771) | | (220,329) |
| Change in Uncollected Customer Payments from Federal Sources | | 133,869 | | 92,421 |
|      Total, Change in Obligated Balance | | 13,432,953 | | 15,214,565 |
| | | | | |
| Obligated Balance, Net, End of Period: | | | | |
|    Unpaid Obligations | | 13,872,909 | | 15,788,389 |
|    Less: Uncollected Customer Payments from Federal Sources | | (439,956) | | (573,824) |
|      Total, Unpaid Obligated Balance, Net, End of Period | $ | 13,432,953 | $ | 15,214,565 |
| | | | | |
| | | | | |
| **NET OUTLAYS** | | | | |
| Net Outlays: | | | | |
|    Gross Outlays (Note 27) | $ | 13,588,391 | $ | 10,670,422 |
|    Less: Offsetting Collections (Note 27) | | (1,189,788) | | (719,558) |
|    Less: Distributed Offsetting Receipts (Notes 27 and 31) | | (1,402,960) | | (1,884,134) |
| **Total, Net Outlays** | $ | 10,995,643 | $ | 8,066,730 |

**The accompanying notes are an integral part of these financial statements.**

# Environmental Protection Agency
## Statements of Custodial Activity
## For the Periods Ending September 30, 2010 and 2009
## (Dollars in Thousands)

|  | FY 2010 | FY 2009 |
|---|---|---|
| **Revenue Activity:** | | |
| Sources of Cash Collections: | | |
| Fines and Penalties | $ 88,318 | $ 101,613 |
| Other | 18,072 | (14,079) |
| Total Cash Collections | $ 106,390 | $ 87,534 |
| Accrual Adjustment | (16,763) | 16,390 |
| Total Custodial Revenue (Note 26) | $ 89,627 | $ 103,924 |
| | | |
| **Disposition of Collections:** | | |
| Transferred to Others (General Fund) | $ 105,684 | $ 87,520 |
| Increases/Decreases in Amounts to be Transferred | (16,057) | 16,404 |
| Total Disposition of Collections | $ 89,627 | $ 103,924 |
| | | |
| **Net Custodial Revenue Activity (Note 26)** | $ - | $ - |

**The accompanying notes are an integral part of these financial statements.**

**Environmental Protection Agency**
**Notes to the Financial Statements**
**Fiscal Year Ended September 30, 2010 and 2009**
**(Dollars in Thousands)**

---

| Note 1. *Summary of Significant Accounting Policies* |
|---|

## A. Reporting Entities

The EPA was created in 1970 by executive reorganization from various components of other federal agencies to better marshal and coordinate federal pollution control efforts. The Agency is generally organized around the media and substances it regulates - air, water, land, hazardous waste, pesticides, and toxic substances.

The FY 2010 financial statements are presented on a consolidated basis for the Balance Sheet, Statements of Net Cost, Changes in Net Position and Custodial Activity and a combined basis for the Statement of Budgetary Resources. These financial statements include the accounts of all funds described in this note by their respective Treasury fund group.

## B. Basis of Presentation

These accompanying financial statements have been prepared to report the financial position and results of operations of the U. S. Environmental Protection Agency (EPA or Agency) as required by the Chief Financial Officers Act of 1990 and the Government Management Reform Act of 1994. The reports have been prepared from the financial system and records of the Agency in accordance with Office of Management and Budget (OMB) Circular No. A-136, *Financial Reporting Requirements*, and the EPA accounting policies, which are summarized in this note. The Statement of Net Cost has been prepared with cost segregated by the Agency's strategic goals.

1. **General Fund Appropriations (Treasury Fund Groups 0000 – 3999)**

   a. ***State and Tribal Assistance Grants (STAG) Appropriation:*** The STAG appropriation, Treasury fund group 0103, provides funds for environmental programs and infrastructure assistance including capitalization grants for State revolving funds and performance partnership grants. Environmental programs and infrastructure supported are: Clean and Safe Water; capitalization grants for the Drinking Water State Revolving Funds; Clean Air; direct grants for Water and Wastewater Infrastructure needs, partnership grants to meet Health Standards, Protect Watersheds, Decrease Wetland Loss, and Address Agricultural and Urban Runoff and Storm Water; Better Waste Management; Preventing Pollution and

Reducing Risk in Communities, Homes, Workplaces and Ecosystems; and Reduction of Global and Cross Border Environmental Risks.

b.  *Science and Technology (S&T) Appropriation:* The S&T appropriation, Treasury fund group 0107, finances salaries, travel, science, technology, research and development activities, including laboratory supplies, certain operating expenses, grants, contracts, intergovernmental agreements, and purchases of scientific equipment. These activities provide the scientific basis for the Agency's regulatory actions. In FY 2010, Superfund research costs were appropriated in Superfund and transferred to S&T to allow for proper accounting of the costs. Environmental scientific and technological activities and programs include Clean Air; Clean and Safe Water; Americans Right to Know about Their Environment; Better Waste Management; Preventing Pollution and Reducing Risk in Communities, Homes, Workplaces, and Ecosystems; and Safe Food.

c.  *Environmental Programs and Management (EPM) Appropriation:* The EPM appropriation, Treasury fund group 0108, includes funds for salaries, travel, contracts, grants, and cooperative agreements for pollution abatement, control, and compliance activities and administrative activities of the Agency's operating programs. Areas supported from this appropriation include: Clean Air, Clean and Safe Water, Land Preservation and Restoration, Healthy Communities and Ecosystems, and Compliance and Environmental Stewardship.

d.  *Buildings and Facilities Appropriation (B&F):* The B&F appropriation, Treasury fund group 0110, provides for the construction, repair, improvement, extension, alteration, and purchase of fixed equipment or facilities that are owned or used by the EPA.

e.  *Office of Inspector General (OIG) Appropriation:* The OIG appropriation, Treasury fund group 0112, provides funds for audit and investigative functions to identify and recommend corrective actions on management and administrative deficiencies that create the conditions for existing or potential instances of fraud, waste and mismanagement. Additional funds for audit and investigative activities associated with the Superfund and the LUST Trust Funds are appropriated under those Trust Fund accounts and transferred to the Office of Inspector General account. The audit function provides contract, internal controls and performance, and financial and grant audit services. The appropriation includes expenses incurred and reimbursed from the appropriated trust funds accounted for under Treasury fund group 8145 and 8153.

f.  *Payments to the Hazardous Substance Superfund Appropriation:* The Payment to the Hazardous Substance Superfund appropriation, Treasury fund group 0250, authorizes appropriations from the General Fund of the Treasury to finance activities conducted through the Hazardous Substance Superfund Program.

**g. *Payments to Leaking Underground Storage Tank Appropriation:*** The Payment to the Leaking Underground Storage Tank appropriation, Treasury fund group 0251, authorizes appropriations from the General Fund of the Treasury to finance activities conducted through the Leaking Underground Storage Tank program.

**h. *Asbestos Loan Program:*** The Asbestos Loan Program is accounted for under Treasury fund group 0118, Program Account, for interest subsidy and administrative support; under Treasury fund group 4322, Financing Account, for loan disbursements, loans receivable and loan collections on post-FY 1991 loans. *The Asbestos Loan Prog*ram was authorized by the Asbestos School Hazard Abatement Act of 1986 to finance control of asbestos building materials in schools. The Program Account 0118 disburses the subsidy to the Financing Fund for increases in the subsidy. The Financing Account 4322 receives the subsidy payment, borrows from Treasury and collects the asbestos loans.

**i. *Allocations and Appropriations Transferred to the Agency:*** The EPA receives allocations or appropriations transferred from other federal agencies.

**j. *Treasury Clearing Accounts:*** The EPA Department of the Treasury Clearing Accounts include: (1) the Budgetary Suspense Account, (2) the Unavailable Check Cancellations and Overpayments Account, and (3) the Undistributed Intra-agency Payments and Collections (IPAC) Account. These are accounted for under Treasury fund groups 3875, 3880 and 3885, respectively.

**k. *General Fund Receipt Accounts:*** General Fund Receipt Accounts include: Hazardous Waste Permits; Miscellaneous Fines, Penalties and Forfeitures; General Fund Interest; Interest from Credit Reform Financing Accounts; Downward Re-estimates of Subsidies; Fees and Other Charges for Administrative and Professional Services; Miscellaneous Recoveries and Refunds and Proceeds of Sales, Personal Property. These accounts are accounted for under Treasury fund groups 0895, 1099, 1435, 1499, 2753.003, 3200, 3220 and 3845, respectively.

**l. *Allocation of Budget Authority:*** EPA is an allocation budget transfer parent to five federal agencies: Department of Interior, Department of Labor, Center for Disease Control, Department of Commerce, and Federal Emergency Management Agency. EPA has an Interagency Agreement or a Memorandum of Understanding (MOU) with each child agency to provide an annual work plan and quarterly progress report containing an accounting of funds obligated in each budget category within 15 days after the end of each quarter. This allows EPA to properly report the financial activity. The allocation transfers are reported in the net cost of operations, changes in net position, balance sheet and budgetary resources where activity is being performed by the receiving Federal entity. In addition, EPA receives allocation transfers, as a child, from the Bureau of Land Management.

2. **Revolving Funds (Treasury Fund Group 4000 – 4999)**

   a. *Reregistration and Expedited Processing Fund:* The Revolving Fund, Treasury fund group 4310, was authorized by the FIFRA of 1972, as amended by the FIFRA Amendments of 1988 and as amended by the Food Quality Protection Act of 1996. Pesticide Maintenance fees are paid by industry to offset the costs of pesticide re-registration and reassessment of tolerances for pesticides used in or on food and animal feed, as required by law.

   b. *Tolerance Revolving Fund:* The Tolerance Revolving Fund, Treasury fund group 4311, was authorized in 1963 for the deposit of tolerance fees. Fees are paid by industry for federal services to set pesticide chemical residue limits in or on food and animal feed. The fees collected prior to January 2, 1997 were accounted for under this fund. Presently these fees are being deposited in the FIFRA fund (see above).

   c. *Asbestos Loan Program:* The Asbestos Loan Program is accounted for under Treasury fund group 4322, Financing Account for loan disbursements, loans receivable and loan collections on post-FY 1991 loans. Refer to General Fund Appropriations paragraph h. for details.

   d. *Working Capital Fund (WCF):* The WCF, Treasury fund group, 4565, includes four activities: computer support services, financial system services, employee relocation services, and postage. The WCF derives revenue from these activities based upon a fee for services. The WCF's customers currently consist primarily of Agency program offices and a small portion from other federal agencies. Accordingly, those revenues generated by the WCF from services provided to Agency program offices and expenses recorded by the program offices for use of such services, along with the related advances/liabilities, are eliminated on consolidation of the financial statements.

3. **Special Funds (Treasury Fund Group 5000 - 5999)**

*Environmental Services Receipt Account:* The Environmental Services Receipt Account authorized by a 1990 act, "To amend the Clean Air Act (P.L. 101-549)," Treasury fund group 5295, was established for the deposit of fee receipts associated with environmental programs, including radon measurement proficiency ratings and training, motor vehicle engine certifications, and water pollution permits. Receipts in this special fund can only be appropriated to the S&T and EPM appropriations to meet the expenses of the programs that generate the receipts if authorized by Congress in the Agency's appropriations bill.

*Exxon Valdez Settlement Fund:* The Exxon Valdez Settlement Fund authorized by a 1992 act, "Making appropriations for the Department of Veterans Affairs and Housing and Urban Development, and for sundry independent agencies, boards, commissions corporations, and offices for the fiscal year ending September 30, 1993 (P.L. 102-389)," Treasury fund group 5297, has funds available to carry out authorized environmental restoration activities. Funding is derived from the collection of reimbursements under the Exxon Valdez settlement as a result of an oil spill.

*Pesticide Registration Fund:* The Pesticide Registration Fund authorized by the "Consolidated Appropriations Act, 2004 (P.L. 108-199)," Treasury fund group 5374, was authorized for the expedited processing of certain registration petitions and associated establishment of tolerances for pesticides to be used in or on food and animal feed. Fees covering these activities, as authorized under the FIFRA Amendments of 1988, are to be paid by industry and deposited into this fund group.

4. **Deposit Funds (Treasury Fund Group 6000 – 6999)**

Deposits include: Fees for Ocean Dumping; Nonconformance Penalties; Clean Air Allowance Auction and Sale; Advances without Orders; and Suspense and Payroll Deposits for Savings Bonds, and State, City Income Taxes Withheld, and Other Federal Payroll Withholding Allotments. These funds are accounted for under Treasury fund groups 6264, 6265, 6266, 6500, 6050, 6275, and 6276, respectively.

5. **Trust Funds (Treasury Fund Group 8000 – 8999)**

   a. ***Superfund Trust Fund:*** In 1980, the Superfund Trust Fund, Treasury fund group 8145, was established by the Comprehensive Environmental Response, Compensation, and Liability Act of 1980 (CERCLA) to provide resources needed to respond to and clean up hazardous substance emergencies and abandoned, uncontrolled hazardous waste sites. The Superfund Trust Fund financing is shared by federal and state governments as well as industry. The EPA allocates funds from its appropriation to other federal agencies to carry out CERCLA. Risks to public health and the environment at uncontrolled hazardous waste sites qualifying for the Agency's National Priorities List (NPL) are reduced and addressed through a process involving site assessment and analysis and the design and implementation of cleanup remedies. NPL cleanups and removals are conducted and financed by the EPA, private parties, or other federal agencies. The Superfund Trust Fund includes Treasury's collections and investment activity.

b. ***Leaking Underground Storage Tank (LUST) Trust Fund:*** The LUST Trust Fund, Treasury fund group 8153, was authorized by the Superfund Amendments and Reauthorization Act of 1986 (SARA) as amended by the Omnibus Budget Reconciliation Act of 1990. The LUST appropriation provides funding to respond to releases from leaking underground petroleum tanks. The Agency oversees cleanup and enforcement programs which are implemented by the states. Funds are allocated to the states through cooperative agreements to clean up those sites posing the greatest threat to human health and the environment. Funds are used for grants to non-state entities including Indian tribes under Section 8001 of the Resource Conservation and Recovery Act. The program is financed by a one cent a gallon tax on motor fuels which will expire in 2011.

c. ***Oil Spill Response Trust Fund:*** The Oil Spill Response Trust Fund, Treasury fund group 8221, was authorized by the Oil Pollution Act of 1990 (OPA). Monies were appropriated to the Oil Spill Response Trust Fund in 1993. The Agency is responsible for directing, monitoring and providing technical assistance for major inland oil spill response activities. This involves setting oil prevention and response standards, initiating enforcement actions for compliance with OPA and Spill Prevention Control and Countermeasure requirements, and directing response actions when appropriate. The Agency carries out research to improve response actions to oil spills including research on the use of remediation techniques such as dispersants and bioremediation. Funding for oil spill cleanup actions is provided through the U.S. Coast Guard under the Oil Spill Liability Trust Fund and reimbursable funding from other federal agencies.

d ***Miscellaneous Contributed Funds Trust Fund:*** The Miscellaneous Contributed Funds Trust Fund authorized in the Federal Water Pollution Control Act (Clean Water Act) as amended by (P.L. 92-500, The Federal Water Pollution Control Act Amendments of 1972), Treasury fund group 8741, includes gifts for pollution control programs that are usually designated for a specific use by donors and/or deposits from pesticide registrants to cover the costs of petition hearings when such hearings result in unfavorable decisions to the petitioner.

## C. Budgets and Budgetary Accounting

### 1. General Funds

Congress adopts an annual appropriation for STAG, B&F, and for Payments to the Hazardous Substance Superfund to be available until expended, as well as annual appropriations for S&T, EPM and for the OIG to be available for 2 fiscal years. When the appropriations for the General Funds are enacted, Treasury issues a warrant to the respective appropriations. As the Agency disburses obligated amounts, the balance of funds available to the appropriation is reduced at Treasury.

The Asbestos Loan Program is a commercial activity financed from a combination of two sources, one for the long term costs of the loans and another for the remaining non-subsidized portion of the loans. Congress adopted a 1 year appropriation, available for obligation in the fiscal year for which it was appropriated, to cover the estimated long term cost of the Asbestos loans. The long term costs are defined as the net present value of the estimated cash flows associated with the loans. The portion of each loan disbursement that did not represent long term cost is financed under permanent indefinite borrowing authority established with the Treasury. A permanent indefinite appropriation is available to finance the costs of subsidy re-estimates that occur in subsequent years after the loans were disbursed.

Funds transferred from other federal agencies are processed as non-expenditure transfers. As the Agency disburses the obligated amounts, the balance of funding available to the appropriation is reduced at Treasury.

Clearing accounts and receipt accounts receive no appropriated funds. Amounts are recorded to the clearing accounts pending further disposition. Amounts recorded to the receipt accounts capture amounts collected for or payable to the Treasury General Fund.

### 2. Revolving Funds

Funding of the FIFRA and Pesticide Registration Funds is provided by fees collected from industry to offset costs incurred by the Agency in carrying out these programs. Each year the Agency submits an apportionment request to OMB based on the anticipated collections of industry fees.

Funding of the WCF is provided by fees collected from other Agency appropriations and other federal agencies to offset costs incurred for providing Agency administrative support for computer and telecommunication services, financial system services, employee relocation services, and postage.

### 3. Special Funds

The Environmental Services Receipt Account obtains fees associated with environmental programs.

Exxon Valdez uses funding collected from reimbursement from the Exxon Valdez settlement.

### 4. Deposit Funds

Deposit accounts receive no appropriated funds. Amounts are recorded to the deposit accounts pending further disposition. These are not EPA's funds.

### 5. Trust Funds

Congress adopts an annual appropriation amount for the Superfund, LUST and the Oil Spill Response Trust Funds to remain available until expended. A transfer account for the Superfund and LUST Trust Fund has been established for purposes of carrying out the program activities. As the Agency disburses obligated amounts from the transfer account, the Agency draws down monies from the Superfund and LUST Trust Fund at Treasury to cover the amounts being disbursed. The Agency draws down all the appropriated monies from the Principal Fund of the Oil Spill Liability Trust Fund when Congress adopts the appropriation amount.

## D. Basis of Accounting

Generally Accepted Accounting Principles (GAAP) for Federal entities is the standard prescribed by the Federal Accounting Standards Advisory Board (FASAB), which is the official standard-setting body for the Federal government. The financial statements are prepared in accordance with GAAP for Federal entities.

Transactions are recorded on an accrual accounting basis and on a budgetary basis (where budgets are issued). Under the accrual method, revenues are recognized when earned and expenses are recognized when a liability is incurred, without regard to receipt or payment of cash. Budgetary accounting facilitates compliance with legal constraints and controls over the use of federal funds.

## E. Revenues and Other Financing Sources

The following EPA policies and procedures to account for inflow of revenue and other financing sources are in accordance with Statement of Federal Financial Accounting Standards (SFFAS) No. 7, "Accounting for Revenues and Other Financing Sources."

The Superfund program receives most of its funding through appropriations that may be used within specific statutory limits for operating and capital expenditures (primarily equipment). Additional financing for the Superfund program is obtained through: reimbursements from other federal agencies, state cost share payments under Superfund State Contracts (SSCs), and settlement proceeds from Potentially Responsible Parties (PRPs) under CERCLA Section 122(b)(3) placed in special accounts. Cost recovery settlements that are not placed in special accounts continue to be deposited in the Trust Fund.

Most of the other funds receive funding needed to support programs through appropriations which may be used within statutory limits for operating and capital expenditures. However, under Credit Reform provisions, the Asbestos Loan Program receives funding to support the subsidy cost of loans through appropriations which may be used within statutory limits. The Asbestos Direct Loan Financing fund 4322, an off-budget fund, receives additional funding to support the outstanding loans through collections from the Program fund 0118 for the subsidized portion of the loan.

The FIFRA and Pesticide Registration funds receive funding through fees collected for services provided and interest on invested funds. The WCF receives revenue through fees collected for services provided to Agency program offices. Such revenue is eliminated with related Agency program expenses upon consolidation of the Agency's financial statements. The Exxon Valdez Settlement Fund receives funding through reimbursements.

Appropriated funds are recognized as Other Financing Sources expended when goods and services have been rendered without regard to payment of cash. Other revenues are recognized when earned (i.e., when services have been rendered).

## F. Funds with the Treasury

The Agency does not maintain cash in commercial bank accounts. Cash receipts and disbursements are handled by Treasury. The major funds maintained with Treasury are Appropriated Funds, Revolving Funds, Trust Funds, Special Funds, Deposit Funds, and Clearing Accounts. These funds have balances available to pay current liabilities and finance authorized obligations, as applicable.

## G. Investments in U.S. Government Securities

Investments in U.S. Government securities are maintained by Treasury and are reported at amortized cost net of unamortized discounts. Discounts are amortized over the term of the investments and reported as interest income. No provision is made for unrealized gains or losses on these securities because, in the majority of cases, they are held to maturity (see Note 4).

## H. Notes Receivable

The Agency records notes receivable at their face value and any accrued interest as of the date of receipt.

## I. Marketable Securities

The Agency records marketable securities at cost as of the date of receipt. Marketable securities are held by Treasury and reported at their cost value in the financial statements until sold (see Note 4).

## J. Accounts Receivable and Interest Receivable

The majority of receivables for non-Superfund funds represent penalties and interest receivable for general fund receipt accounts, unbilled intragovernmental reimbursements receivable, allocations receivable from Superfund (eliminated in consolidated totals), and refunds receivable for the STAG appropriation.

Superfund accounts receivable represent recovery of costs from PRPs as provided under CERCLA as amended by SARA. Since there is no assurance that these funds will be recovered, cost recovery expenditures are expensed when incurred (see Note 5).

The Agency records accounts receivable from PRPs for Superfund site response costs when a consent decree, judgment, administrative order, or settlement is entered. These agreements are generally negotiated after at least some, but not necessarily all, of the site response costs have been incurred. It is the Agency's position that until a consent decree or other form of settlement is obtained, the amount recoverable should not be recorded.

The Agency also records accounts receivable from states for a percentage of Superfund site remedial action costs incurred by the Agency within those states. As agreed to under SSCs, cost sharing arrangements may vary according to whether a site was privately or publicly operated at the time of hazardous substance disposal and whether the Agency response action was removal or remedial. SSC agreements are usually for 10 percent or 50 percent of site remedial action costs, depending on who has the lead for the site (i.e., publicly or privately owned). States may pay the full amount of their share in advance or incrementally throughout the remedial action process.

## K. Advances and Prepayments

Advances and prepayments represent funds advanced or prepaid to other entities both internal and external to the Agency for which a budgetary expenditure has not yet occurred.

## L. Loans Receivable

Loans are accounted for as receivables after funds have been disbursed. Loans receivable resulting from obligations on or before September 30, 1991, are reduced by the allowance for uncollectible loans. Loans receivable resulting from loans obligated on or after October 1, 1991, are reduced by an allowance equal to the present value of the subsidy costs associated with these loans. The subsidy cost is calculated based on the interest rate differential between the loans and Treasury borrowing, the estimated delinquencies and defaults net of recoveries offset by fees collected and other estimated cash flows associated with these loans.

## M. Appropriated Amounts Held by Treasury

For the Superfund and LUST Trust Funds and for amounts appropriated from the Superfund Trust Fund to the OIG, cash available to the Agency that is not needed immediately for current disbursements remains in the respective Trust Funds managed by Treasury.

## N. Property, Plant, and Equipment

EPA accounts for its personal and real property accounting records in accordance with SFFAS No. 6, "Accounting for Property, Plant and Equipment." For EPA-held property, the Fixed Assets Subsystem (FAS) automatically generates depreciation entries monthly based on acquisition dates.

A purchase of EPA-held or contract personal property is capitalized if it is valued at $25 thousand or more and has an estimated useful life of at least 2 years. For contractor held property, depreciation is taken on a modified straight-line basis over a period of 6 years depreciating 10 percent the first and sixth year, and 20 percent in years 2 through 5. Detailed records are maintained and accounted for in contractor systems, not in FAS for contractor held property. Acquisitions of EPA-held personal property are depreciated using the straight-line method over the specific asset's useful life, ranging from 2 to 15 years.

Personal property also consists of capital leases. To be defined as a capital lease, it must, at its inception, have a lease term of two or more years and the lower of the fair value or present value of the minimum lease payments must be $75 thousand or more. Capital leases may also contain real property (therefore considered in the real property category as well), but these need to meet an $85 thousand capitalization threshold. In addition, the lease must meet one of the following criteria: transfers ownership to EPA, contains a bargain purchase option, the lease term is equal to 75 percent or more of the estimated service life, or the present value of the lease and other minimum lease payments equal or exceed 90 percent of the fair value.

Superfund contract property used as part of the remedy for site-specific response actions is capitalized in accordance with the Agency's capitalization threshold. This property is part of the remedy at the site and eventually becomes part of the site itself. Once the response action has been completed and the remedy implemented, EPA retains control of the property (i.e., pump and treat facility) for 10 years or less, and transfers its interest in the facility to the respective state for mandatory operation and maintenance – usually 20 years or more. Consistent with EPA's 10 year retention period, depreciation for this property is based on a 10 year life. However, if any property is transferred to a state in a year or less, this property is charged to expense. If any property is sold prior to EPA relinquishing interest, the proceeds from the sale of that property shall be applied against contract payments or refunded as required by the Federal Acquisition Regulations.

An exception to the accounting of contract property includes equipment purchased by the Working Capital Fund (WCF). This property is retained in FAS and depreciated utilizing the straight-line method based upon the asset's acquisition date and useful life.

Real property consists of land, buildings, capital and leasehold improvements and capital leases. Real property, other than land, is capitalized when the value is $85 thousand or more. Land is capitalized regardless of cost. Buildings are valued at an estimated original cost basis, and land is valued at fair market value if purchased prior to FY 1997. Real property purchased during and after FY 1997 is valued at actual cost. Depreciation for real property is calculated using the straight-line method over the specific asset's useful life, ranging from 10 to 102 years. Leasehold improvements are amortized over the lesser of their useful life or the unexpired lease term. Additions to property and improvements not meeting the capitalization criteria, expenditures for minor alterations, and repairs and maintenance are expensed when incurred.

Software for the WCF, a revenue generating activity, is capitalized if the purchase price is $100 thousand or more with an estimated useful life of 2 years or more. All other funds capitalize software if those investments are considered Capital Planning and Investment Control (CPIC) or CPIC Lite systems with the provisions of SFFAS No. 10, "Accounting for Internal Use Software." Once software enters the production life cycle phase, it is depreciated using the straight-line method over the specific asset's useful life ranging from 2 to 10 years.

## O. Liabilities

Liabilities represent the amount of monies or other resources that are more likely than not to be paid by the Agency as the result of an Agency transaction or event that has already occurred and can be reasonably estimated. However, no liability can be paid by the Agency without an appropriation or other collections. Liabilities for which an appropriation has not been enacted are classified as unfunded liabilities and there is no certainty that the appropriations will be enacted. Liabilities of the Agency arising from other than contracts can be abrogated by the Government acting in its sovereign capacity.

## P. Borrowing Payable to the Treasury

Borrowing payable to Treasury results from loans from Treasury to fund the Asbestos direct loans described in part B. and C. of this note. Periodic principal payments are made to Treasury based on the collections of loans receivable.

## Q. Interest Payable to Treasury

The Asbestos Loan Program makes periodic interest payments to Treasury based on its debt.

## R. Accrued Unfunded Annual Leave

Annual, sick and other leave is expensed as taken during the fiscal year. Sick leave earned but not taken is not accrued as a liability. Annual leave earned but not taken as of the end of the fiscal year is accrued as an unfunded liability. Accrued unfunded annual leave is included in Note 34 as a component of "Payroll and Benefits Payable."

## S. Retirement Plan

There are two primary retirement systems for federal employees. Employees hired prior to January 1, 1987, may participate in the Civil Service Retirement System (CSRS). On January 1, 1984, the Federal Employees Retirement System (FERS) went into effect pursuant to Public Law 99-335. Most employees hired after December 31, 1983, are automatically covered by FERS and Social Security. Employees hired prior to January 1, 1984, elected to either join FERS and Social Security or remain in CSRS. A primary feature of FERS is that it offers a savings plan to which the Agency automatically contributes one percent of pay and matches any employee contributions up to an additional four percent of pay. The Agency also contributes the employer's matching share for Social Security.

With the issuance of SFFAS No. 5, "Accounting for Liabilities of the Federal Government," accounting and reporting standards were established for liabilities relating to the federal employee benefit programs (Retirement, Health Benefits, and Life

Insurance). SFFAS No. 5 requires that the employing agencies recognize the cost of pensions and other retirement benefits during their employees' active years of service. SFFAS No. 5 requires that the Office of Personnel Management (OPM), as administrator of the CSRS and FERS, the Federal Employees Health Benefits Program, and the Federal Employees Group Life Insurance Program, provide federal agencies with the actuarial cost factors to compute the liability for each program.

## T. Prior Period Adjustments and Restatements

Prior period adjustments, if any, are made in accordance with SFFAS No. 21, "Reporting Corrections of Errors and Changes in Accounting Principles." Specifically, prior period adjustments will only be made for material prior period errors to: (1) the current period financial statements, and (2) the prior period financial statements presented for comparison. Adjustments related to changes in accounting principles will only be made to the current period financial statements, but not to prior period financial statements presented for comparison.

## U. Recovery Act Funds

On February 17, 2009, President Obama signed the American Recovery and Reinvestment Act of 2009 (Recovery Act). The Act was enacted to create jobs in the United States, encourage technical advances, assist in modernizing the nation's infrastructure, and enhance energy independence. The EPA was charged with the task of distributing funds to invest in various projects aimed at creating advances in science, health, and environmental protection that will provide long-term economic benefits.

EPA manages almost $7.22 billion in Recovery Act funded projects and programs that will help achieve these goals, offer resources to help other "green" agencies, and administer environmental laws that will govern Recovery activities. As of September 30, 2010, EPA has paid out $3.71 billion.

EPA, in collaboration with states, tribes, local governments, territories and other partners, is administering the funds it received under the Recovery Act through four appropriations. The funds include:

State and Tribal Assistance Grants (STAG) that in turn include: $4 billion for assistance to help communities with water quality and wastewater infrastructure needs and $2 billion for drinking water infrastructure needs (Water State Revolving Fund programs and Water Quality Planning program); $100 million for competitive grants to evaluate and clean up former industrial and commercial sites (Brownfields program); $300 million for grants and loans to help regional, state and local governments, tribal agencies, and non-profit organizations with projects that reduce diesel emissions (Clean Diesel programs); $600 million for the cleanup of hazardous sites (Superfund program); $200 million for cleanup of petroleum leaks from underground storage tanks (Leaking Underground Storage Tank Fund program); and $20 million for audits and investigations conducted by the Inspector General (IG).

The EPA has committed to focusing on the following areas: Clean Diesel Emissions, Superfund Hazardous Waste Cleanup, Cleaner Underground Storage Tank Sites, Revitalized Neighborhoods from Brownfields and Cleaner Water and Drinking Water Infrastructures.

The vast majority of the contracts awarded under the Recovery Act will be entered into using competitive contracts. EPA is committed fully to ensuring transparency and accountability throughout the Agency in spending Recovery Act funds in accordance with OMB guidance.

EPA has set up a Stimulus Steering Committee that meets to review and report on the status of the distribution of the Recovery Act Funds to ensure transparency and accuracy. EPA has also developed a Stewardship Plan which is an Agency-level risk mitigation plan that sets out the Agency's Recovery Act risk assessment, internal controls and monitoring activities. The Stewardship Plan is divided into seven functional areas: grants, interagency agreements, contracts, human capital/payroll, budget execution, performance reporting and financial reporting. The Stewardship Plan was developed around Government Accountability Office (GAO) standards for internal control. Under each functional area, risks are assessed and related control, communication and monitoring activities are identified for each impacted program. The Plan is a dynamic document and will be updated as revised OMB guidance is issued or additional risks are uncovered.

EPA has the three-year EPM treasury symbol 689/10108 that is under the Recovery Act. EPA's two-year EPM treasury symbol 689/00108 is a "regular" program. EPA's other Recovery Act programs are the following:  Office of Inspector General, treasury symbol 689/20113; State and Tribal Assistance Grants, treasury symbol 689/00102; Payment to the Superfund, treasury symbol 689/00249; Superfund, treasury symbol 689/08195; and Leaking Underground Storage Tank, treasury symbol 689/08196.

## V. British Petroleum (BP) Oil Spill

On April 20, 2010 the Deepwater Horizon drilling rig exploded, releasing large volumes of oil into the Gulf of Mexico. As a responsible party, BP is required by the 1990 Oil Pollution Act to fund the cost of the response and cleanup operations.  EPA has been working in conjunction with the Coast Guard who was named the lead on the effort to fund the immediate oil spill clean ups.

## W. Use of Estimates

The preparation of financial statements requires management to make certain estimates and assumptions that affect the reported amounts of assets and liabilities and the reported amounts of revenue and expenses during the reporting period. Actual results could differ from those estimates.

### Note 2. Fund Balance with Treasury (FBWT)

Fund Balance with Treasury as of September 30, 2010 and 2009, consists of the following:

| | FY 2010 Entity Assets | FY 2010 Non-Entity Assets | Total | FY 2009 Entity Assets | FY 2009 Non-Entity Assets | Total |
|---|---|---|---|---|---|---|
| **Trust Funds:** | | | | | | |
| Superfund | $ 106,247 | $ - | $ 106,247 | $ 62,631 | $ - | $ 62,631 |
| LUST | 55,132 | - | 55,132 | 25,169 | - | 25,169 |
| Oil Spill & Misc | 9,644 | - | 9,644 | 2,441 | - | 2,441 |
| **Revolving Funds:** | | | | | | |
| FIFRA/Tolerance | 4,204 | - | 4,204 | 7,153 | - | 7,153 |
| Working Capital | 80,485 | - | 80,485 | 80,293 | - | 80,293 |
| Cr Reform Finan | 390 | - | 390 | 390 | - | 390 |
| **Appropriated** | 14,049,511 | - | 14,049,511 | 15,122,481 | - | 15,122,481 |
| **Other Fund Types** | 289,149 | 8,262 | 297,411 | 247,877 | 9,482 | 257,359 |
| **Total** | $ 14,594,762 | $ 8,262 | $ 14,603,024 | $ 15,548,435 | $ 9,482 | $ 15,557,917 |

Entity fund balances, except for special fund receipt accounts, are available to pay current liabilities and to finance authorized purchase commitments (see Status of Fund Balances below). Entity Assets for Other Fund Types consist of special purpose funds and special fund receipt accounts, such as the Pesticide Registration funds and the Environmental Services receipt account. The Non-Entity Assets for Other Fund Types consist of clearing accounts and deposit funds, which are either awaiting documentation for the determination of proper disposition or being held by EPA for other entities.

| Status of Fund Balances: | FY 2010 | FY 2009 |
|---|---|---|
| Unobligated Amounts in Fund Balance: | | |
| Available for Obligation | $ 4,430,813 | $ 3,440,831 |
| Unavailable for Obligation | 195,529 | 262,971 |
| Net Receivables from Invested Balances | (3,736,818) | (3,583,119) |
| Balances in Treasury Trust Fund (Note 38) | (1,115) | (18,334) |
| Obligated Balance not yet Disbursed | 13,432,954 | 15,214,555 |
| Non-Budgetary FBWT | 281,661 | 241,013 |
| **Totals** | $ 14,603,024 | $ 15,557,917 |

The funds available for obligation may be apportioned by OMB for new obligations at the beginning of the following fiscal year. Funds unavailable for obligation are mostly balances in expired funds, which are available only for adjustments of existing obligations. For FY 2010 and FY 2009 no differences existed between Treasury's accounts and EPA's statements for fund balances with Treasury.

## Note 3. Cash and Other Monetary Assets

As of September 30, 2010 and 2009, the balance in the imprest fund was $10 thousand.

## Note 4. Investments

As of September 30, 2010 and 2009 investments related to Superfund and LUST consist of the following:

| | | Cost | | Amortized (Premium) Discount | | Interest Receivable | | Investments, Net | | Market Value |
|---|---|---|---|---|---|---|---|---|---|---|
| Intragovernmental Securities: | | | | | | | | | | |
| Non-Marketable | FY 2010 | $ 7,079,053 | $ | (139,302) | $ | 25,258 | $ | 7,243,613 | $ | 7,243,613 |
| Non-Marketable | FY 2009 | $ 6,641,708 | $ | (195,777) | $ | 42,463 | $ | 6,879,948 | $ | 6,879,948 |

CERCLA, as amended by SARA, authorizes EPA to recover monies to clean up Superfund sites from responsible parties (RPs). Some RPs file for bankruptcy under Title 11 of the U.S. Code. In bankruptcy settlements, EPA is an unsecured creditor and is entitled to receive a percentage of the assets remaining after secured creditors have been satisfied. Some RPs satisfy their debts by issuing securities of the reorganized company. The Agency does not intend to exercise ownership rights to these securities, and instead will convert them to cash as soon as practicable (see Note 6). All investments in Treasury securities are earmarked funds (see Note 19).

The Federal Government does not set aside assets to pay future benefits or other expenditures associated with earmarked funds. The cash receipts collected from the public for an earmarked fund are deposited in the U.S. Treasury, which uses the cash for general Government purposes. Treasury securities are issued to EPA as evidence of its receipts. Treasury securities are an asset to EPA and a liability to the U.S. Treasury. Because EPA and the U.S. Treasury are both parts of the Government, these assets and liabilities offset each other from the standpoint of the Government as a whole. For this reason, they do not represent an asset or liability in the U.S. Government-wide financial statements.

Treasury securities provide EPA with authority to draw upon the U.S. Treasury to make future benefit payments or other expenditures. When EPA requires redemption of these securities to make expenditures, the Government finances those expenditures out of accumulated cash balances, by raising taxes or other receipts, by borrowing from the public or repaying less debt, or by curtailing other expenditures. This is the same way that the Government finances all other expenditures.

## Note 5. Accounts Receivable, Net

The Accounts Receivable as of September 30, 2010 and 2009 consist of the following:

| | | FY 2010 | | FY 2009 |
|---|---|---|---|---|
| **Intragovernmental:** | | | | |
| Accounts & Interest Receivable | $ | 45,698 | $ | 39,362 |
| Total | $ | 45,698 | $ | 39,362 |
| | | | | |
| **Non-Federal:** | | | | |
| Unbilled Accounts Receivable | $ | 143,444 | $ | 137,593 |
| Accounts & Interest Receivable | | 1,958,981 | | 1,376,831 |
| Less: Allowance for Uncollectibles | | (1,684,890) | | (696,580) |
| Total | $ | 417,535 | $ | 817,844 |

The Allowance for Uncollectible Accounts is determined both on a specific identification basis, as a result of a case-by-case review of receivables, and on a percentage basis for receivables not specifically identified.

## Note 6. Other Assets

Other Assets as of September 30, 2010 and 2009 consist of the following:

| **Intragovernmental:** | | FY 2010 | | FY 2009 |
|---|---|---|---|---|
| Advances to Federal Agencies | $ | 223,165 | $ | 214,654 |
| Advances for Postage | | 131 | | 177 |
| Total | $ | 223,296 | $ | 214,831 |
| | | | | |
| **Non-Federal:** | | | | |
| Travel Advances | $ | 432 | $ | (183) |
| Letter of Credit Advances | | 9 | | 8 |
| Other Advances | | 2,105 | | 2,146 |
| Operating Materials and Supplies | | 149 | | 147 |
| Inventory for Sale | | 139 | | 110 |
| Total | $ | 2,834 | $ | 2,228 |

## Note 7. Loans Receivable, Net

Loans Receivable consists of Asbestos Loan Program loans disbursed from obligations made prior to FY 1992 and are presented net of allowances for estimated uncollectible loans, if an allowance was considered necessary. Loans disbursed from obligations made after FY 1991 are governed by the Federal Credit Reform Act, which mandates that the present value of the subsidy costs (i.e., interest rate differentials, interest subsidies, anticipated delinquencies, and defaults) associated with direct loans be recognized as an expense in the year the loan is made. The net loan present value is the gross loan receivable less the subsidy present value. The amounts as of September 30, 2010 and 2009 are as follows:

| | FY 2010 | | | FY 2009 | | |
| | Loans Receivable, Gross | Allowance* | Value of Assets Related to Direct Loans | Loans Receivable, Gross | Allowance* | Value of Assets Related to Direct Loans |
|---|---|---|---|---|---|---|
| Direct Loans Obligated Prior to FY 1992 | $ 545 | $ - | $ 545 | $ 2,003 | $ - | $ 2,003 |
| Direct Loans Obligated After FY 1991 | 4,931 | (222) | 4,709 | 10,590 | (948) | 9,642 |
| Total | $ 5,476 | $ (222) | $ 5,254 | $ 12,593 | $ (948) | $ 11,645 |

* Allowance for Pre-Credit Reform loans (prior to FY 1992) is the Allowance for Estimated Uncollectible Loans, and the Allowance for Post Credit Reform Loans (after FY 1991) is the Allowance for Subsidy Cost (present value).

During FY 2008, EPA made a payment within the U.S. Treasury for the Asbestos Loan Program based on an upward re-estimate of $33 thousand for increased loan financing costs. It was believed that the payment only consisted of "interest" costs and, as such, an automatic apportionment, per OMB Circular A-11, Section 120.83, was deemed appropriate. However, approximately one third ($12 thousand) of the $33 thousand re-estimate was for increased "subsidy" costs which requires an approved apportionment by OMB before any payment could be made. Therefore, the payment resulted in a minor technical Anti-deficiency Act (ADA) violation. On October 13, 2009, EPA transmitted, as required by OMB Circular A-11, Section 145, written notifications to the (1) President, (2) President of the Senate, (3) Speaker of the House of Representatives, (4) Comptroller General, and (5) the Director of OMB.

## Subsidy Expenses for Credit Reform Loans (reported on a cash basis):

| | Interest Rate Re-estimate | Technical Re-estimate | Total |
|---|---|---|---|
| Upward Subsidy Reestimate – FY 2010 | $ 5 $ | 2 $ | 7 |
| Downward Subsidy Reestimate - FY 2010 | (35) | (16) | (51) |
| **FY 2010 Totals** | $ **(30)** $ | **(14)** $ | **(44)** |
| | | | |
| Upward Subsidy Reestimate – FY 2009 | $ - $ | - $ | - |
| Downward Subsidy Reestimate - FY 2009 | (3) | (2) | (5) |
| **FY 2009 Totals** | $ **(3)** $ | **(2)** $ | **(5)** |

### Schedule for Reconciling Subsidy Cost Allowance Balances
### (Post-1991 Direct Loans)

| | FY 2010 | FY 2009 |
|---|---|---|
| Beginning balance of the subsidy cost allowance | $ (948) | $ (1,752) |
| Add: subsidy expense for direct loans disbursed during the reporting years by component: | | |
| Interest rate differential costs | | |
| Default costs (net of recoveries) | | |
| Fees and other collections | | |
| Other subsidy costs | | |
| Total of the above subsidy expense components | $ - | $ - |
| Adjustments: | | |
| Loan Modification | | |
| Fees received | | |
| Foreclosed property acquired | | |
| Loans written off | | 1 |
| Subsidy allowance amortization | 477 | 752 |
| Other | | |
| End balance of the subsidy cost allowance before reestimates | 477 | 753 |
| Add or subtract subsidy reestimates by component: | | |
| (a) Interest rate reestimate | 176 | 36 |
| (b) Technical/default reestimate | 73 | 15 |
| Total of the above reestimate components | 249 | 51 |
| **Ending Balance of the subsidy cost allowance** | $ (222) | $ (948) |

EPA has not disbursed Direct Loans since 1993.

## Note 8. Accounts Payable and Accrued Liabilities

The Accounts Payable and Accrued Liabilities are current liabilities and consist of the following amounts as of September 30, 2010 and 2009:

| | | FY 2010 | | FY 2009 |
|---|---|---|---|---|
| **Intragovernmental:** | | | | |
| Accounts Payable | $ | 1,466 | $ | 2,230 |
| Accrued Liabilities | | 49,859 | | 73,824 |
| Total | $ | **51,325** | $ | **76,054** |
| | | | | |
| **Non-Federal:** | | **FY 2010** | | **FY 2009** |
| Accounts Payable | $ | 118,033 | $ | 116,799 |
| Advances Payable | | 8 | | 9 |
| Interest Payable | | 7 | | 6 |
| Grant Liabilities | | 650,526 | | 521,188 |
| Other Accrued Liabilities | | 262,874 | | 227,762 |
| Total | $ | **1,031,448** | $ | **865,764** |

Other Accrued Liabilities primarily relate to contractor accruals.

## Note 9. General Property, Plant, and Equipment, Net

General property, plant, and equipment (PP&E) consist of software, real property, EPA and contractor-held personal property, and capital leases.

As of September 30, 2010 and 2009, General PP&E consist of the following:

| | | FY 2010 | | | FY 2009 | |
|---|---|---|---|---|---|---|
| | Acquisition Value | Accumulated Depreciation | Net Book Value | Acquisition Value | Accumulated Depreciation | Net Book Value |
| EPA-Held Equipment | $ 252,920 $ | (145,672) $ | 107,248 $ | 246,999 $ | (138,385) $ | 108,614 |
| Software | 443,847 | (158,034) | 285,813 | 373,964 | (118,115) | 255,849 |
| Contractor Held Equip. | 95,494 | (39,225) | 56,269 | 79,855 | (47,207) | 32,648 |
| Land and Buildings | 630,252 | (177,654) | 452,598 | 607,131 | (166,316) | 440,815 |
| Capital Leases | 35,440 | (22,247) | 13,193 | 41,068 | (26,506) | 14,562 |
| Total | $ **1,457,953** $ | **(542,832)** $ | **915,121** $ | **1,349,017** $ | **(496,529)** $ | **852,488** |

## Note 10. Debt Due to Treasury

The debt due to Treasury consists of borrowings to finance the Asbestos Loan Program. The debt to Treasury as of September 30, 2010 and 2009 is as follows:

| All Other Funds | | FY 2010 | | | FY 2009 | |
|---|---|---|---|---|---|---|
| | Beginning Balance | Net Borrowing | Ending Balance | Beginning Balance | Net Borrowing | Ending Balance |
| **Intragovernmental:** | | | | | | |
| Debt to Treasury | $ 9,983 | $ (5,139) | $ 4,844 | $ 13,158 | $ (3,175) | $ 9,983 |

## Note 11. Stewardship Land

The Agency acquires title to certain property and property rights under the authorities provided in Section 104(j) CERCLA related to remedial clean-up sites. The property rights are in the form of fee interests (ownership) and easements to allow access to clean-up sites or to restrict usage of remediated sites. The Agency takes title to the land during remediation and transfers it to state or local governments upon the completion of clean-up. A site with "land acquired" may have more than one acquisition property. Sites are not counted as a withdrawal until all acquired properties have been transferred under the terms of 104(j).

As of September 30, 2010, the Agency possesses the following land and land rights:

| | FY 2010 | FY 2009 |
|---|---|---|
| **Superfund Sites with Easements** | | |
| Beginning Balance | 33 | 32 |
| Additions | 2 | 2 |
| Withdrawls | 0 | 1 |
| Ending Balance | 35 | 33 |
| | | |
| **Superfund Sites with Land Acquired** | | |
| Beginning Balance | 30 | 31 |
| Additions | 2 | 0 |
| Withdrawls | 0 | 1 |
| Ending Balance | 32 | 30 |

## Note 12.  Custodial Liability

Custodial Liability represents the amount of net accounts receivable that, when collected, will be deposited to the Treasury General Fund.  Included in the custodial liability are amounts for fines and penalties, interest assessments, repayments of loans, and miscellaneous other accounts receivable.  As of September 30, 2010 and 2009, custodial liability is approximately $53 million and $71 million, respectively.

## Note 13. Other Liabilities

Other Liabilities consist of the following as of September 30, 2010:

| Other Liabilities – Intragovernmental | Covered by Budgetary Resources | Not Covered by Budgetary Resources | Total |
|---|---|---|---|
| **Current** | | | |
| Employer Contributions & Payroll Taxes | $ 22,585 | $ - | $ 22,585 |
| WCF Advances | 1,706 | - | 1,706 |
| Other Advances | 52,596 | - | 52,596 |
| Advances, HRSTF Cashout | 20,431 | - | 20,431 |
| Deferred HRSTF Cashout | 1,831 | - | 1,831 |
| Liability for Deposit Funds | - | - | - |
| Resources Payable to Treasury | 649 | - | 649 |
| Subsidy Payable to Treasury | 256 | - | 256 |
| **Non-Current** | | | |
| Unfunded FECA Liability | - | 10,232 | 10,232 |
| Payable to Treasury Judgment Fund | - | 22,000 | 22,000 |
| **Total Intragovernmental** | $ 100,054 | $ 32,232 | $ 132,286 |
| | | | |
| **Other Liabilities - Non-Federal** | | | |
| **Current** | | | |
| Unearned Advances, Non-Federal | $ 65,314 | $ - | $ 65,314 |
| Liability for Deposit Funds, Non-Federal | 8,128 | - | 8,128 |
| Contract Holdbacks | 155 | | 155 |
| **Non-Current** | | | |
| Other Liabilities | - | 200 | 200 |
| Capital Lease Liability | - | 26,199 | 26,199 |
| **Total Non-Federal** | $ 73,597 | $ 26,399 | $ 99,996 |

Other Liabilities consist of the following as of September 30, 2009:

| Other Liabilities – Intragovernmental | Covered by Budgetary Resources | | Not Covered by Budgetary Resources | | Total |
|---|---|---|---|---|---|
| **Current** | | | | | |
| Employer Contributions & Payroll Taxes | $ | 19,875 | $ | - | $ 19,875 |
| WCF Advances | | 960 | | - | 960 |
| Other Advances | | 60,043 | | - | 60,043 |
| Advances, HRSTF Cashout | | 27,642 | | - | 27,642 |
| Deferred HRSTF Cashout | | - | | - | - |
| Liability for Deposit Funds | | - | | - | - |
| Resources Payable to Treasury | | 3 | | - | 3 |
| Subsidy Payable to Treasury | | 54 | | - | 54 |
| **Non-Current** | | | | | - |
| Unfunded FECA Liability | | - | | 10,068 | 10,068 |
| Payable to Treasury Judgment Fund | | - | | 22,000 | 22,000 |
| **Total Intragovernmental** | $ | **108,577** | $ | **32,068** | $ **140,645** |
| | | | | | |
| **Other Liabilities - Non-Federal** | | | | | |
| **Current** | | | | | |
| Unearned Advances | $ | 79,490 | $ | - | $ 79,490 |
| Liability for Deposit Funds | | 8,330 | | - | 8,330 |
| **Non-Current** | | | | | - |
| Other Liabilities | | - | | 230 | 230 |
| Capital Lease Liability | | - | | 27,868 | 27,868 |
| **Total Non-Federal** | $ | **87,820** | $ | **28,098** | $ **115,918** |

---

## Note 14. Leases

### Capital Leases:

The value of assets held under Capital Leases as of September 30, 2010 and 2009 are as follows:

| Summary of Assets Under Capital Lease: | | FY 2010 | | FY 2009 |
|---|---|---|---|---|
| Real Property | $ | 35,285 | $ | 40,913 |
| Personal Property | | 155 | | 155 |
| Software License | | | | - |
| **Total** | $ | **35,440** | $ | **41,068** |
| Accumulated Amortization | $ | 22,246 | $ | 26,506 |

EPA had three capital leases for land and buildings housing scientific laboratories and computer facilities. All of these leases include a base rental charge and escalation clauses based upon either rising operating costs and/or real estate taxes. The base operating costs are adjusted annually according to escalators in the Consumer Price Indices published by the Bureau of Labor Statistics, U.S. Department of Labor. One capital lease expired during FY 2010 and the others leases terminate in FY 2013 and FY 2025.

The total future minimum capital lease payments are listed below.

**Future Payments Due:**

| Fiscal Year | | Capital Leases |
|---|---|---|
| 2011 | $ | 5,714 |
| 2012 | | 5,714 |
| 2013 | | 5,714 |
| 2014 | | 4,215 |
| After 5 years | | 43,558 |
| **Total Future Minimum Lease Payments** | | 64,915 |
| Less: Imputed Interest | $ | (38,716) |
| **Net Capital Lease Liability** | | 26,199 |
| **Liabilities not Covered by Budgetary Resources** | $ | **26,199** |

(See Note 13)

## Operating Leases:

The GSA provides leased real property (land and buildings) as office space for EPA employees. GSA charges a Standard Level User Charge that approximates the commercial rental rates for similar properties.

EPA had four direct operating leases for land and buildings housing scientific laboratories and computer facilities. The leases include a base rental charge and escalation clauses based upon either rising operating costs and/or real estate taxes. The base operating costs are adjusted annually according to escalators in the Consumer Price Indices published by the Bureau of Labor Statistics. Two leases expired in FY 2010 and the other two expire in FY 2017 and FY 2020. These charges are expended from the EPM appropriation.

The total minimum future operating lease costs are listed below:

| Fiscal Year | | Operating Leases, Land and Buildings |
|---|---|---|
| 2011 | $ | 89 |
| 2012 | | 89 |
| 2013 | | 89 |
| 2014 | | 89 |
| Beyond 2014 | | 374 |
| | | |
| **Total Future Minimum Lease Payments** | $ | **730** |

## Note 15. FECA Actuarial Liabilities

The Federal Employees' Compensation Act (FECA) provides income and medical cost protection to covered Federal civilian employees injured on the job, employees who have incurred a work-related occupational disease, and beneficiaries of employees whose death is attributable to a job-related injury or occupational disease. Annually, EPA is allocated the portion of the long term FECA actuarial liability attributable to the entity. The liability is calculated to estimate the expected liability for death, disability, medical and miscellaneous costs for approved compensation cases. The liability amounts and the calculation methodologies are provided by the Department of Labor.

The FECA Actuarial Liability as of September 30, 2010 and 2009 was $44.9 million and $44.1 million, respectively. The FY 2010 present value of these estimated outflows is calculated using a discount rate of 3.653 percent in the first year, and 4.3 percent in the years thereafter. The estimated future costs are recorded as an unfunded liability.

## Note 16. Cashout Advances, Superfund

Cashout advances are funds received by EPA, a state, or another PRP under the terms of a settlement agreement (e.g., consent decree) to finance response action costs at a specified Superfund site. Under CERCLA Section 122(b)(3), cashout funds received by EPA are placed in site-specific, interest bearing accounts known as special accounts and are used for potential future work at such sites in accordance with the terms of the settlement agreement. Funds placed in special accounts may be disbursed to PRPs, to states that take responsibility for the site, or to other Federal agencies to conduct or finance response actions in lieu of EPA without further appropriation by Congress. As of September 30, 2010 and 2009, cashouts are approximately $637 million and $572 million respectively.

## Note 17. Unexpended Appropriations – Other Funds

As of September 30, 2010 and 2009, the Unexpended Appropriations consist of the following:

| Unexpended Appropriations: | | FY 2010 | | FY 2009 |
|---|---|---|---|---|
| Unobligated | | | | |
| Available | $ | 184,815 | $ | 1,652,461 |
| Unavailable | | 275,592 | | 70,053 |
| Undelivered Orders | | 12,882,377 | | 12,813,833 |
| Total | $ | 13,342,784 | $ | 14,536,347 |

## Note 18. Commitments and Contingencies

EPA may be a party in various administrative proceedings, actions and claims brought by or against it. These include:

- Various personnel actions, suits, or claims brought against the Agency by employees and others.
- Various contract and assistance program claims brought against the Agency by vendors, grantees and others.
- The legal recovery of Superfund costs incurred for pollution cleanup of specific sites, to include the collection of fines and penalties from responsible parties.
- Claims against recipients for improperly spent assistance funds which may be settled by a reduction of future EPA funding to the grantee or the provision of additional grantee matching funds.

As of September 30, 2010 and 2009 total accrued liabilities for commitments and potential loss contingencies is $4.37 million and $4.57 million, respectively. Further discussion of the cases and claims that give rise to this accrued liability are discussed immediately below.

**Litigation Claims and Assessments**

There is currently one legal claim which has been asserted against the EPA pursuant to the Federal Tort Claims and Fair Labor Standards Acts. This loss has been deemed probable, and the unfavorable outcome is estimated to be between $2 million and $8 million. EPA has accrued the higher conservative amount as of September 30, 2010. The maximum amount of exposure under the claim could range as much as $8 million in the aggregate.

**Superfund**

Under CERCLA Section 106(a), EPA issues administrative orders that require parties to clean up contaminated sites. CERCLA Section 106(b) allows a party that has complied with such an order to petition EPA for reimbursement from the fund of its reasonable costs of responding to the order, plus interest. To be eligible for reimbursement, the party must demonstrate either that it was not a liable party under CERCLA Section 107(a) for the response action ordered, or that the Agency's selection of the response action was arbitrary and capricious or otherwise not in accordance with law.

As of September 30, 2010, there is one CERCLA Section 106(b) administrative claim which has been asserted and for which an unfavorable outcome has been deemed probable. It is estimated that the potential loss could be approximately $2.37 million and this amount has been accrued as of September 30, 2010.

**Judgment Fund**

In cases that are paid by the U.S. Treasury Judgment Fund, EPA must recognize the full cost of a claim regardless of which entity is actually paying the claim. Until these claims are settled or a court judgment is assessed and the Judgment Fund is determined to be the appropriate source for the payment, claims that are probable and estimable must be recognized as an expense and liability of the Agency. For these cases, at the time of settlement or judgment, the liability will be reduced and an imputed financing source recognized. See Interpretation of Federal Financial Accounting Standards No. 2, "Accounting for Treasury Judgment Fund Transactions."

As of September 30, 2010, there are no material claims pending in the Treasury's Judgment Fund. However, EPA has a $22 million liability to the Treasury Judgment Fund for a payment made by the Fund to settle a contract dispute claim.

**Other Commitments**

EPA has a commitment to fund the United States Government's payment to the Commission of the North American Agreement on Environmental Cooperation between the Governments of Canada, the Government of the United Mexican States, and the Government of the United States of America (commonly referred to as CEC). According to the terms of the agreement, each government pays an equal share to cover the operating costs of the CEC. For the periods ended September 30, 2010 and 2009, EPA paid $3 million for each of these periods to the CEC. A payment of $3 million was made in FY 2010.

EPA has a legal commitment under a non-cancellable agreement, subject to the availability of funds, with the United Nations Environment Program (UNEP). This agreement enables EPA to provide funding to the Multilateral Fund for the Implementation of the Montreal Protocol. EPA made payments totaling $10.5 million in FY 2010. Future payments totaling

$9.6 million have been deemed reasonably possible and are anticipated to be paid in fiscal years 2011 through 2013.

## Note 19. Earmarked Funds

| Balance sheet as of September 30, 2010 | Environmental Services | LUST | Superfund | Other Earmarked Funds | Total Earmarked Funds |
|---|---|---|---|---|---|
| **Assets** | | | | | |
| Fund Balance with Treasury | $ 273,420 | $ 55,132 | $ 106,247 | $ 29,578 | $ 464,377 |
| Investments | | 3,502,913 | 3,740,700 | | 7,243,613 |
| Accounts Receivable, Net | | | 391,388 | 7,697 | 399,085 |
| Other Assets | | 266 | 115,729 | 6,199 | 122,194 |
| Total Assets | 273,420 | 3,558,311 | 4,354,064 | 43,474 | 8,229,269 |
| | | | | | |
| Other Liabilities | $ 4 | $ 19,094 | $ 1,013,566 | $ 44,223 | $ 1,076,887 |
| Total Liabilities | $ 4 | $ 19,094 | $ 1,013,566 | $ 44,223 | $ 1,076,887 |
| | | | | | |
| Cumulative Results of Operations | $ 273,416 | $ 3,539,217 | $ 3,340,498 | $ (749) | $ 7,152,382 |
| | | | | | |
| Total Liabilities and Net Position | $ 273,420 | $ 3,558,311 | $ 4,354,064 | $ 43,474 | $ 8,229,269 |
| | | | | | |
| **Statement of Changes in Net Cost for the Period Ended September 30, 2010** | | | | | |
| Gross Program Costs | $ - | $ 181,870 | $ 1,844,712 | $ 121,214 | $ 2,147,796 |
| Less: Earned Revenues | - | | 484,165 | 98,246 | 582,411 |
| | | | | | |
| Net Cost of Operations | $ - | $ 181,870 | $ 1,360,547 | $ 22,968 | $ 1,565,385 |
| | | | | | |
| | | | | | |
| **Statement of Changes in Net Position for the Period ended September 30, 2010** | | | | | |
| Net Position, Beginning of Period | $ 231,820 | $ 3,436,303 | $ 3,416,536 | $ 1,817 | $ 7,086,476 |
| Nonexchange Revenue- Securities Investments | | 115,523 | 14,968 | 13 | 130,504 |
| Nonexchange Revenue | 41,596 | 168,990 | 3,396 | 2 | 213,984 |
| Other Budgetary Finance Sources | | | 1,241,402 | 18,379 | 1,259,781 |
| Other Financing Sources | | 271 | 24,743 | 2,008 | 27,022 |
| Net Cost of Operations | | (181,870) | (1,360,547) | (22,968) | (1,565,385) |
| | | | | | |
| Change in Net Position | $ 41,596 | $ 102,914 | $ (76,038) | $ (2,566) | $ 65,906 |
| | | | | | |
| Net Position | $ 273,416 | $ 3,539,217 | $ 3,340,498 | $ (749) | $ 7,152,382 |

| Balance sheet as of September 30, 2009 | Environmental Services | LUST | Superfund | Other Earmarked Funds | Total Earmarked Funds |
|---|---|---|---|---|---|
| **Assets** | | | | | |
| Fund Balance with Treasury | $ 231,821 | $ 25,169 | $ 62,631 | $ 25,650 | $ 345,271 |
| Investments | - | 3,422,610 | 3,457,338 | - | 6,879,948 |
| Accounts Receivable, Net | - | - | 769,531 | 4,157 | 773,688 |
| Other Assets | - | 217 | 104,735 | 4,827 | 109,780 |
| Total Assets | 231,821 | 3,447,996 | 4,394,236 | 34,635 | 8,108,687 |
| | | | | | |
| Other Liabilities | $ 1 | $ 11,693 | $ 977,700 | $ 32,817 | $ 1,022,211 |
| Total Liabilities | $ 1 | $ 11,693 | $ 977,700 | $ 32,817 | $ 1,022,211 |
| | | | | | |
| Cumulative Results of Operations | $ 231,820 | $ 3,436,303 | $ 3,416,536 | $ 1,817 | $ 7,086,476 |
| | | | | | |
| Total Liabilities and Net Position | $ 231,821 | $ 3,447,996 | $ 4,394,236 | $ 34,634 | $ 8,108,687 |
| | | | | | |
| **Statement of Net Cost for the Period Ended September 30, 2009** | | | | | |
| Gross Program Costs | $ - | $ 98,901 | $ 1,672,246 | $ 75,485 | $ 1,846,632 |
| Less: Earned Revenues | - | 79 | 615,577 | 55,411 | 671,067 |
| Net Cost of Operations | $ - | $ 98,822 | $ 1,056,669 | $ 20,074 | $ 1,175,565 |
| | | | | | |
| **Statement of Changes in Net Position for the Period ended September 30, 2009** | | | | | |
| Net Position, Beginning of Period | $ 211,282 | $ 3,244,497 | $ 2,702,763 | $ 1,989 | $ 6,160,531 |
| Nonexchange Revenue- Securities Investments | - | 124,088 | 52,065 | 15 | 176,168 |
| Nonexchange Revenue | 20,538 | 169,186 | (1,479) | - | 188,245 |
| Other Budgetary Finance Sources | - | (3,000) | 1,693,519 | 17,687 | 1,708,206 |
| Other Financing Sources | - | 354 | 26,338 | 2,199 | 28,891 |
| Net Cost of Operations | - | (98,822) | (1,056,669) | (20,074) | (1,175,565) |
| Change in Net Position | $ 20,538 | $ 191,806 | $ 713,774 | $ (173) | $ 925,945 |
| | | | | | |
| Net Position | $ 231,820 | $ 3,436,303 | $ 3,416,537 | $ 1,816 | $ 7,086,476 |

## Earmarked funds are as follows:

***Environmental Services Receipt Account:*** The Environmental Services Receipt Account authorized by a 1990 act, "To amend the Clean Air Act (P.L. 101-549)," Treasury fund group 5295, was established for the deposit of fee receipts associated with environmental programs, including radon measurement proficiency ratings and training, motor vehicle engine certifications, and water pollution permits. Receipts in this special fund can only be appropriated to the S&T and EPM appropriations to meet the expenses of the programs that generate the receipts if authorized by Congress in the Agency's appropriations bill.

***Leaking Underground Storage Tank (LUST) Trust Fund:*** The LUST Trust Fund, Treasury fund group 8153, was authorized by the Superfund Amendments and Reauthorization Act of 1986 (SARA) as amended by the Omnibus Budget Reconciliation Act of 1990. The LUST appropriation provides funding to respond to releases from leaking underground petroleum tanks. The Agency oversees cleanup and enforcement programs which are implemented by the states. Funds are allocated to the states through cooperative agreements to clean up those sites posing the greatest threat to human health and the environment. Funds are used for grants to non-state entities including Indian tribes under Section 8001 of the Resource

Conservation and Recovery Act. The program is financed by a one cent per gallon tax on motor fuels which will expire in 2011.

*Superfund Trust Fund:* In 1980, the Superfund Trust Fund, Treasury fund group 8145, was established by CERCLA to provide resources to respond to and clean up hazardous substance emergencies and abandoned, uncontrolled hazardous waste sites. The Superfund Trust Fund financing is shared by federal and state governments as well as industry. The EPA allocates funds from its appropriation to other Federal agencies to carry out CERCLA. Risks to public health and the environment at uncontrolled hazardous waste sites qualifying for the Agency's National Priorities List (NPL) are reduced and addressed through a process involving site assessment and analysis and the design and implementation of cleanup remedies. NPL cleanups and removals are conducted and financed by the EPA, private parties, or other Federal agencies. The Superfund Trust Fund includes Treasury's collections, special account receipts from settlement agreements, and investment activity.

**Other Earmarked Funds**:

*Oil Spill Response Trust Fund:* The Oil Spill Response Trust Fund, Treasury fund group 8221, was authorized by the Oil Pollution Act of 1990 (OPA). Monies were appropriated to the Oil Spill Response Trust Fund in 1993. The Agency is responsible for directing, monitoring and providing technical assistance for major inland oil spill response activities. This involves setting oil prevention and response standards, initiating enforcement actions for compliance with OPA and Spill Prevention Control and Countermeasure requirements, and directing response actions when appropriate. The Agency carries out research to improve response actions to oil spills including research on the use of remediation techniques such as dispersants and bioremediation. Funding for oil spill cleanup actions is provided through the U.S. Coast Guard under the Oil Spill Liability Trust Fund and reimbursable funding from other Federal agencies.

*Miscellaneous Contributed Funds Trust Fund:* The Miscellaneous Contributed Funds Trust Fund authorized in the Federal Water Pollution Control Act (Clean Water Act) as amended P.L. 92-500 (The Federal Water Pollution Control Act Amendments of 1972), Treasury fund group 8741, includes gifts for pollution control programs that are usually designated for a specific use by donors and/or deposits from pesticide registrants to cover the costs of petition hearings when such hearings result in unfavorable decisions to the petitioner.

*Pesticide Registration Fund:* The Pesticide Registration Fund authorized by a 2004 Act, "Consolidated Appropriations Act (P.L. 108-199)," Treasury fund group 5374, was authorized in 2004 for the expedited processing of certain registration petitions and associated establishment of tolerances for pesticides to be used in or on food and animal feed. Fees covering these activities, as authorized under the FIFRA Amendments of 1988, are to be paid by industry and deposited into this fund group.

*Reregistration and Expedited Processing Fund:* The Revolving Fund, Treasury fund group 4310, was authorized by the FIFRA of 1972, as amended by the FIFRA Amendments of 1988 and as amended by the Food Quality Protection Act of 1996. Pesticide maintenance fees are paid by industry to offset the costs of pesticide re-registration and reassessment of tolerances for pesticides used in or on food and animal feed, as required by law.

*Tolerance Revolving Fund:* The Tolerance Revolving Fund, Treasury fund group 4311, was authorized in 1963 for the deposit of tolerance fees. Fees are paid by industry for Federal services to set pesticide chemical residue limits in or on food and animal feed. The fees collected prior to January 2, 1997 were accounted for under this fund. Presently collection of these fees is prohibited by statute, enacted in the Consolidated Appropriations Act, 2004 (P.L. 108-199).

*Exxon Valdez Settlement Fund:* The Exxon Valdez Settlement Fund authorized by P.L. 102-389, "Making appropriations for the Department of Veterans Affairs and Housing and Urban Development, and for sundry independent agencies, boards, commissions, corporations, and offices for the fiscal year ending September 30, 1993," Treasury fund group 5297, has funds available to carry out authorized environmental restoration activities. Funding is derived from the collection of reimbursements under the Exxon Valdez settlement as a result of an oil spill.

---

### Note 20. Exchange Revenues, Statement of Net Cost

---

Exchange, or earned revenues on the Statement of Net Cost include income from services provided, interest revenue (with the exception of interest earned on trust fund investments), and miscellaneous earned revenue. As of September 30, 2010 and 2009, exchange revenues are $693.4 million and $773.6 million respectively.

## Note 21. Intragovernmental Costs and Exchange Revenue

| | FY 2010 | | | FY 2009 | | |
|---|---|---|---|---|---|---|
| | Intragovernmental | With the Public | Total | Intragovernmental | With the Public | Total |
| **Clean Air** | | | | | | |
| Program Costs | $ 170,677 | $ 1,048,124 | $ 1,218,801 | $ 187,484 | $ 874,787 | $ 1,062,271 |
| Earned Revenue | 18,923 | 5,906 | 24,829 | 15,455 | 3,036 | 18,491 |
| NET COST | $ 151,754 | $ 1,042,218 | $ 1,193,972 | $ 172,029 | $ 871,751 | $ 1,043,780 |
| **Clean and Safe Water** | | | | | | |
| Program Costs | $ 193,456 | $ 6,197,330 | $ 6,390,786 | $ 191,558 | $ 3,236,903 | $ 3,428,461 |
| Earned Revenue | 2,803 | 2,524 | 5,327 | 4,758 | 3,208 | 7,966 |
| NET COSTS | $ 190,653 | $ 6,194,806 | $ 6,385,459 | $ 186,800 | $ 3,233,695 | $ 3,420,495 |
| **Land Preservation & Restoration** | | | | | | |
| Program Costs | $ 342,734 | $ 2,096,211 | $ 2,438,945 | $ 386,549 | $ 1,821,301 | $ 2,207,850 |
| Earned Revenue | 103,687 | 446,569 | 550,256 | 101,767 | 580,119 | 681,886 |
| NET COSTS | $ 239,047 | $ 1,649,642 | $ 1,888,689 | $ 284,782 | $ 1,241,182 | $ 1,525,964 |
| **Healthy Communities & Ecosystems** | | | | | | |
| Program Costs | $ 293,850 | $ 1,265,653 | $ 1,559,503 | $ 271,028 | $ 1,134,155 | $ 1,405,183 |
| Earned Revenue | 64,034 | 44,144 | 108,178 | 20,047 | 42,267 | 62,314 |
| NET COSTS | $ 229,816 | $ 1,221,509 | $ 1,451,325 | $ 250,981 | $ 1,091,888 | $ 1,342,869 |
| **Compliance & Environmental Stewardship** | | | | | | |
| Program Costs | $ 182,299 | $ 615,931 | $ 798,230 | $ 207,660 | $ 609,538 | $ 817,198 |
| Earned Revenue | 3,400 | 1,494 | 4,894 | 4,071 | (1,116) | 2,955 |
| NET COSTS | $ 178,899 | $ 614,437 | $ 793,336 | $ 203,589 | $ 610,654 | $ 814,243 |
| **Total** | | | | | | |
| Program Costs | $ 1,183,016 | $ 11,223,249 | $ 12,406,265 | $ 1,244,279 | $ 7,676,684 | $ 8,920,963 |
| Earned Revenue | 192,847 | 500,637 | 693,484 | 146,098 | 627,514 | 773,612 |
| NET COSTS | $ 990,169 | $ 10,722,612 | $ 11,712,781 | $ 1,098,181 | $ 7,049,170 | $ 8,147,351 |

Intragovernmental costs relate to the source of goods or services not the classification of the related revenue.

## Note 22. Cost of Stewardship Land

There were no costs related to the acquisition of stewardship land for September 30, 2010 and approximately $323 thousand for September 30, 2009. These costs are included in the Statement of Net Cost.

## Note 23. Environmental Cleanup Costs

As of September 30, 2010, EPA has one site that requires clean up stemming from its activities. For sites that had previously been listed, it was determined by EPA's Office of

General Counsel to discontinue reporting the potential environmental liabilities for the following reasons: (1) although EPA has been put on notice that it is subject to a contribution claim under CERCLA, no direct demand for compensation has been made to EPA; (2) any demand against EPA will be resolved only after the Superfund cleanup work is completed, which may be years in the future; and (3) there was no legal activity on these matters in FY2009 or in FY2010. During FY2009, costs amounting to approximately $53 thousand were paid out by the Treasury Judgment Fund for another site, and no further action is warranted.

EPA also holds title to a site in Edison, New Jersey which was formerly an Army Depot. While EPA did not cause the contamination, the Agency could potentially be liable for a portion of the cleanup costs, an unfunded environmental liability of $200 thousand.

Accrued Cleanup Cost:

EPA has 15 sites that will require permanent closure, and EPA is responsible to fund the environmental cleanup of those sites. As of September 30, 2010 and 2009, the estimated costs for site cleanup were $20.15 million and $19.49 million, respectively. Since the cleanup costs associated with permanent closure were not primarily recovered through user fees, EPA has elected to recognize the estimated total cleanup cost as a liability and record changes to the estimate in subsequent years.

## Note 24. State Credits

Authorizing statutory language for Superfund and related Federal regulations requires states to enter into Superfund State Contracts (SSC) when EPA assumes the lead for a remedial action in their state. The SSC defines the state's role in the remedial action and obtains the state's assurance that it will share in the cost of the remedial action. Under Superfund's authorizing statutory language, states will provide EPA with a 10 percent cost share for remedial action costs incurred at privately owned or operated sites, and at least 50 percent of all response activities (i.e., removal, remedial planning, remedial action, and enforcement) at publicly operated sites. In some cases, states may use EPA-approved credits to reduce all or part of their cost share requirement that would otherwise be borne by the states. The credit is limited to state site-specific expenses EPA has determined to be reasonable, documented, direct out-of-pocket expenditures of non-Federal funds for remedial action.

Once EPA has reviewed and approved a state's claim for credit, the state must first apply the credit at the site where it was earned. The state may apply any excess/remaining credit to another site when approved by EPA. As of September 30, 2010 and 2009, the total remaining state credits have been estimated at $21.0 million and $21.9 million, respectively.

## Note 25. Preauthorized Mixed Funding Agreements

Under Superfund preauthorized mixed funding agreements, PRPs agree to perform response actions at their sites with the understanding that EPA will reimburse them a certain percentage of their total response action costs. EPA's authority to enter into mixed funding agreements is provided under CERCLA Section 111(a)(2). Under CERCLA Section 122(b)(1), as amended by SARA, PRPs may assert a claim against the Superfund Trust Fund for a portion of the costs they incurred while conducting a preauthorized response action agreed to under a mixed funding agreement. As of September 30, 2010, EPA had 6 outstanding preauthorized mixed funding agreements with obligations totaling $15.6 million. As of September 30, 2009, EPA had 9 for $19.9 million. A liability is not recognized for these amounts until all work has been performed by the PRP and has been approved by EPA for payment. Further, EPA will not disburse any funds under these agreements until the PRP's application, claim, and claims adjustment processes have been reviewed and approved by EPA.

## Note 26. Custodial Revenues and Accounts Receivable

|  | FY 2010 | FY 2009 |
|---|---|---|
| Fines, Penalties and Other Miscellaneous Receipts | $ 89,627 | $ 103,924 |
| Accounts Receivable for Fines, Penalties and Other Miscellaneous Receipts: |  |  |
| Accounts Receivable | $ 229,658 | $ 238,957 |
| Less: Allowance for Uncollectible Accounts | (181,153) | (174,411) |
| Total | $ 48,505 | $ 64,546 |

EPA uses the accrual basis of accounting for the collection of fines, penalties and miscellaneous receipts. Collectability by EPA of the fines and penalties is based on the PRPs' willingness and ability to pay.

## Note 27. Reconciliation of President's Budget to the Statement of Budgetary Resources

Budgetary resources, obligations incurred and outlays, as presented in the audited FY 2010 Statement of Budgetary Resources will be reconciled to the amounts included in the FY 2011 Budget of the United States Government when they become available. The Budget of the United States Government with actual numbers for FY 2010 has not yet been published. We expect it will be published by early 2011, and it will be available on the OMB website at http://www.whitehouse.gov/.

The actual amounts published for the year ended September 30, 2009 are listed immediately below:

| FY 2009 | | Budgetary Resources | Obligations | Offsetting Receipts | Net Outlays |
|---|---|---|---|---|---|
| Statement of Budgetary Resources | $ | 21,014,069 | $ 17,311,047 | $ 1,884,134 | $ 9,950,864 |
| Adjustments to Undelivered Orders and Others | | 844 | (404) | | (2) |
| Expired and Immaterial Funds* | | (251,035) | (37) | | 5 |
| Rounding Differences** | | (8,878) | (5,606) | (134) | 133 |
| Reported in Budget of the U. S. Government | $ | 20,755,000 | $ 17,305,000 | $ 1,884,000 | $ 9,951,000 |

* Expired funds are not included in Budgetary Resources Available for Obligation and Total New Obligations in the Budget Appendix (lines 23.90 and 10.00). Also, minor funds are not included in the Budget Appendix.
** Balances are rounded to millions in the Budget Appendix.

## Note 28. Recoveries and Resources Not Available, Statement of Budgetary Resources

Recoveries of Prior Year Obligations, Temporarily Not Available, and Permanently Not Available on the Statement of Budgetary Resources consist of the following amounts for September 30, 2010 and 2009:

| | | FY 2010 | | FY 2009 |
|---|---|---|---|---|
| Recoveries of Prior Year Obligations - Downward adjustments of prior years' obligations | $ | 277,771 | $ | 220,329 |
| Temporarily Not Available - Rescinded Authority | | (11,800) | | - |
| Permanently Not Available: | | | | |
| Payments to Treasury | | (5,191) | | (3,180) |
| Rescinded authority | | (52,897) | | (10,000) |
| Canceled authority | | (15,365) | | (19,552) |
| Total Permanently Not Available | $ | (73,453) | $ | (32,732) |

## Note 29. Unobligated Balances Available

Unobligated balances are a combination of two lines on the Statement of Budgetary Resources: Apportioned, Unobligated Balances and Unobligated Balances Not Available. Unexpired unobligated balances are available to be apportioned by the OMB for new obligations at the beginning of the following fiscal year. The expired unobligated balances are only available for upward adjustments of existing obligations.

The unobligated balances available consist of the following as of September 30, 2010 and 2009:

| | | FY 2010 | | FY 2009 |
|---|---|---|---|---|
| Unexpired Unobligated Balance | $ | 4,441,115 | $ | 3,452,750 |
| Expired Unobligated Balance | | 185,226 | | 250,272 |
| **Total** | $ | **4,626,341** | $ | **3,703,022** |

## Note 30. Undelivered Orders at the End of the Period

Budgetary resources obligated for undelivered orders at September 30, 2010 and 2009 were $12.63 billion and $14.69 billion, respectively.

## Note 31. Offsetting Receipts

Distributed offsetting receipts credited to the general fund, special fund, or trust fund receipt accounts offset gross outlays. For FY 2010 and 2009, the following receipts were generated from these activities:

| | | FY 2010 | | FY 2009 |
|---|---|---|---|---|
| Trust Fund Recoveries | $ | 53,247 | $ | 96,782 |
| Special Fund Environmental Service | | 41,599 | | 20,539 |
| Downward Re-estimates of Subsidies | | 51 | | 5 |
| Trust Fund Appropriation | | 1,280,570 | | 1,747,911 |
| Special Fund Receipt Account and Treasury | | | | |
| Miscellaneous Receipt and Clearing Accounts | | 27,493 | | 18,897 |
| **Total** | $ | **1,402,960** | $ | **1,884,134** |

## Note 32. Transfers-In and Out, Statement of Changes in Net Position

**Appropriation Transfers, In/Out:**

For FY 2010 and 2009, the Appropriation Transfers under Budgetary Financing Sources on the Statement of Changes in Net Position are comprised of non-expenditure transfers that affect Unexpended Appropriations for non-invested appropriations. These amounts are included in the Budget Authority, Net Transfers and Prior Year Unobligated Balance, Net Transfers lines on the Statement of Budgetary Resources. Details of the Appropriation Transfers on the Statement of Changes in Net Position and reconciliation with the Statement of Budgetary Resources follows for September 30, 2010 and 2009:

**Transfers In/Out Without Reimbursement, Budgetary:**

| Fund/Type of Account | | FY 2010 | FY 2009 |
|---|---|---|---|
| Army Corps of Engineers | $ | (9,000) $ | |
| U.S. Navy | | (8,000) | (8,000) |
| Small Business Administration | | | (2,953) |
| Total Appropriation Transfers (Other Funds) | | (17,000) | (10,953) |
| Net Transfers from Invested Funds | | 1,386,345 | 1,382,030 |
| Transfers to Another Agency | | (17,000) | (10,953) |
| Allocations Rescinded | $ | $ | - |
| Total of Net Transfers on Statement of Budgetary Resources | $ | **1,369,345** $ | **1,371,077** |

For FY 2010 and 2009, Transfers In/Out under Budgetary Financing Sources on the Statement of Changes in Net Position consist of transfers to or from other Federal agencies and between EPA funds. These transfers affect Cumulative Results of Operations. Details of the transfers-in and transfers-out, expenditure and nonexpenditure, follows for September 30, 2010 and 2009:

| Type of Transfer/Funds | | FY 2010 | | | FY 2009 | |
|---|---|---|---|---|---|---|
| | | Earmarked | Other Funds | | Earmarked | Other Funds |
| Transfers-in (out) nonexpenditure, Earmark to S&T and OIG funds | $ | (39,168) $ | 33,859 $ | | (57,392) $ | 57,392 |
| Transfer-in nonexpenditure recovery from CDC | | | | | - | - |
| Transfers-in nonexpenditure, Oil Spill | | 18,379 | | | 17,687 | - |
| Transfer-in (out) cancelled funds | | | | | - | - |
| Total Transfer in (out) without Reimbursement, Budgetary | $ | **(20,789)** $ | **33,859** $ | | **(39,705)** $ | **57,392** |

**Transfers In/Out without Reimbursement, Other Financing Sources:**

For FY 2010 and 2009, Transfers In/Out without Reimbursement under Other Financing Sources on the Statement of Changes in Net Position are comprised of negative subsidy to a special receipt fund for the credit reform funds.

The amounts reported on the Statement of Changes in Net Position are as follows for September 30, 2010 and 2009:

| Type of Transfer/Funds | FY 2010 | | FY 2009 | |
| --- | --- | --- | --- | --- |
| | Earmark | Other Funds | Earmark | Other Funds |
| Transfers-in by allocation transfer agency | $ | $ | $ 84 | $ - |
| Transfers-in property | | 341 | - | 46 |
| Transfers (out) of prior year negative subsidy to be paid following year | | 205 | - | (740) |
| Total Transfer in (out) without Reimbursement, Budgetary | $ - | $ 546 | $ 84 | $ (694) |

---

## Note 33. Imputed Financing

In accordance with SFFAS No. 5, "Accounting for Liabilities of the Federal Government," Federal agencies must recognize the portion of employees' pensions and other retirement benefits to be paid by the OPM trust funds. These amounts are recorded as imputed costs and imputed financing for each agency. Each year the OPM provides Federal agencies with cost factors to calculate these imputed costs and financing that apply to the current year. These cost factors are multiplied by the current year's salaries or number of employees, as applicable, to provide an estimate of the imputed financing that the OPM trust funds will provide for each agency. The estimates for FY 2010 were $146.8 million ($23.7 million from Earmarked funds, and $123.1 million from Other Funds). For FY 2009, the estimates were $197.8 million ($25.1 million from Earmarked funds, and $172.7 million from Other Funds).

SFFAS No. 4, "Managerial Cost Accounting Standards and Concepts" and SFFAS No. 30, "Inter-Entity Cost Implementation," requires Federal agencies to recognize the costs of goods and services received from other Federal entities that are not fully reimbursed, if material. EPA estimates imputed costs for inter-entity transactions that are not at full cost and records imputed costs and financing for these unreimbursed costs subject to materiality. EPA applies its Headquarters General and Administrative indirect cost rate to expenses incurred for inter-entity transactions for which other Federal agencies did not include indirect costs to estimate the amount of unreimbursed (i.e., imputed) costs. For FY 2010 total imputed costs were $10.8 million ($3.3 million from Earmarked funds, and $7.5 million from Other Funds).

In addition to the pension and retirement benefits described above, EPA also records imputed costs and financing for Treasury Judgment Fund payments made on behalf of the Agency. Entries are made in accordance with the Interpretation of Federal Financial Accounting Standards No. 2, "Accounting for Treasury Judgment Fund Transactions." For FY 2010 entries for Judgment Fund payments totaled $4.0 million (Other Funds).  For FY 2009, entries for Judgment Fund payments totaled $3.7 million (Other Funds).

The combined total of imputed financing sources for FY 2010 and FY 2009 is $161.6 million and $213.3 million, respectively.

| Note 34. Payroll and Benefits Payable |
| --- |

Payroll and benefits payable to EPA employees for the years ending September 30, 2010 and 2009 consist of the following:

| FY 2010 Payroll & Benefits Payable | | Covered by Budgetary Resources | | Not Covered by Budgetary Resources | | Total |
| --- | --- | --- | --- | --- | --- | --- |
| Accrued Funded Payroll & Benefits | $ | 66,677 | $ | - | $ | 66,677 |
| Withholdings Payable | | 31,298 | | - | | 31,298 |
| Employer Contributions Payable-TSP | | 3,588 | | - | | 3,588 |
| Accrued Unfunded Annual Leave | | - | | 163,412 | | 163,412 |
| Total - Current | $ | 101,563 | $ | 163,412 | $ | 264,975 |
| | | | | | | |
| FY 2009 Payroll & Benefits Payable | | | | | | |
| Accrued Funded Payroll and Benefits | $ | 57,004 | $ | - | $ | 57,004 |
| Withholdings Payable | | 31,307 | | - | | 31,307 |
| Employer Contributions Payable-TSP | | 3,177 | | - | | 3,177 |
| Accrued Unfunded Annual Leave | | - | | 159,129 | | 159,129 |
| Total - Current | $ | 91,488 | $ | 159,129 | $ | 250,617 |

| Note 35. Other Adjustments, Statement of Changes in Net Position |
| --- |

The Other Adjustments under Budgetary Financing Sources on the Statement of Changes in Net Position consist of rescissions to appropriated funds and cancellation of funds that expired 5 years earlier. These amounts affect Unexpended Appropriations.

| | | Other Funds FY 2010 | | Other Funds FY 2009 |
| --- | --- | --- | --- | --- |
| Rescissions to General Appropriations | $ | 50,623 | $ | 29,551 |
| Canceled General Authority | | 15,366 | | - |
| Total Other Adjustments | $ | 65,989 | $ | 29,551 |

## Note 36. Non-exchange Revenue, Statement of Changes in Net Position

Non-exchange Revenue, Budgetary Financing Sources, on the Statement of Changes in Net Position as of September 30, 2010 and 2009 consists of the following items:

| | | Earmarked Funds FY 2010 | Earmarked Funds FY 2009 |
|---|---|---|---|
| Interest on Trust Fund | $ | 130,504 $ | 176,168 |
| Tax Revenue, Net of Refunds | | 172,127 | 169,186 |
| Fines and Penalties Revenue | | 261 | (1,479) |
| Special Receipt Fund Revenue | | 41,596 | 20,538 |
| **Total Nonexchange Revenue** | $ | **344,488** $ | **364,413** |

## Note 37. Reconciliation of Net Cost of Operations to Budget

| | | FY 2010 | | FY 2009 |
|---|---|---|---|---|
| **RESOURCES USED TO FINANCE ACTIVITIES** | | | | |
| Budgetary Resources Obligated | | | | |
| Obligations Incurred | $ | 11,950,681 | $ | 17,311,047 |
| Less: Spending Athority from Offsetting Collections and Recoveries | | (1,333,690) | | (847,465) |
| Obligations, Net of Offsetting Collections | $ | 10,616,991 | $ | 16,463,582 |
| Less: Offsetting Reciepts | | (1,375,422) | | (1,884,134) |
| Net Obligations | $ | 9,241,569 | $ | 14,579,448 |
| Other Resources | | | | |
| Transfers In/Out without Reimbursement, Property | $ | (341) | $ | 656 |
| Imputed Financing Sources | | 161,640 | | 213,331 |
| Net Other Resources Used to Finance Activities | $ | 161,299 | $ | 213,987 |
| | | | | |
| Total Resources Used to Finance Activities | $ | 9,402,868 | $ | 14,793,435 |
| | | | | |
| **RESOURCES USED TO FINANCE ITEMS** | | | | |
| **NOT PART OF THE NEST COST OF OPERATIONS:** | | | | |
| Change in Budgetary Resources Obligated | $ | 2,166,944 | $ | (6,440,873) |
| Resources that Fund Prior Periods Expenses | | - | | (381) |
| Budgetary Offsetting Collections and Receipts that | | | | |
| Do Not Affect Net Cost of Operations: | | | | |
| Credit Program Collections Increasing Loan Liabilities for | | | | |
| Guarantees or Subsidy Allowances: | | 5,681 | | 3,943 |
| Offsetting Reciepts Not Affecting Net Cost | | 94,852 | | 136,222 |
| Resources that Finance Asset Acquition | | (213,953) | | (138,030) |
| | | | | |
| Total Resources Used to Finance Items Not Part of the Net Cost of Operations | $ | 2,053,524 | $ | (6,439,119) |
| | | | | |
| Total Resources Used to Finance the Net Cost of Operations | $ | 11,456,392 | $ | 8,354,316 |

| | | FY 2010 | | FY 2009 |
|---|---|---|---|---|
| **COMPONENTS OF THE NET COST OF OPERATIONS THAT WILL** | | | | |
| **NOT REQUIRE OR GENERATE RESOURCES IN THE CURRENT PERIOD:** | | | | |
| Components Requiring or Generating Resources in Future Periods: | | | | |
| Increase in Annual Leave Liability | $ | 4,232 | $ | 6,461 |
| Increase in Environmental and Disposal Liability | | 630 | | 83 |
| Increase in Unfunded Contingencies | | (200) | | 4,529 |
| Upward/ Downward Reestimates of Credit Subsidy Expense | | (207) | | - |
| Increase in Public Exchange Revenue Receivables | | 7,375 | | (337,008) |
| Increase in Workers Compensation Costs | | 979 | | - |
| Other | | (3,077) | | (3,232) |
| Total Components of Net Cost of Operations that Require or | | | | |
| Generate Resources in Future Periods | $ | 9,732 | $ | (329,167) |
| | | | | |
| Components Not Requiring/ Generating Resources: | | | | |
| Depreciation and Amortization | | 85,741 | $ | 71,550 |
| Expenses Not Requiring Budgetary Resources | | 160,916 | | 50,652 |
| Total Components of Net Cost that Will Not Require or Generate Resources | $ | 246,657 | $ | 122,202 |
| | | | | |
| Total Components of Net Cost of Operations That Will Not Require or | $ | 256,389 | $ | (206,965) |
| Generate Resources in the Current Period | | | | |
| | | | | |
| **Net Cost of Operations** | $ | 11,712,781 | $ | 8,147,351 |

Amounts held by Treasury for future appropriations consist of amounts held in trusteeship by Treasury in the Superfund and LUST Trust Funds.

**Superfund**

Superfund is supported by general revenues, cost recoveries of funds spent to clean up hazardous waste sites, interest income, and fines and penalties.

The following reflects the Superfund Trust Fund maintained by Treasury as of September 30, 2010 and 2009. The amounts contained in these notes have been provided by Treasury. As indicated, a portion of the outlays represents amounts received by EPA's Superfund Trust Fund; such funds are eliminated on consolidation with the Superfund Trust Fund maintained by Treasury.

| SUPERFUND FY 2010 | EPA | Treasury | Combined |
|---|---|---|---|
| **Undistributed Balances** | | | |
| Uninvested Fund Balance | $ - | $ 4,234,294 | $ 4,234,294 |
| Total Undisbursed Balance | - | 4,234,294 | 4,234,294 |
| Interest Receivable | - | 4,442,724 | 4,442,724 |
| Investments, Net | 3,526,671,825 | 209,585,595 | 3,736,257,420 |
| **Total Assets** | $ 3,526,671,825 | $ 218,262,613 | $ 3,744,934,438 |
| | | | |
| **Liabilities & Equity** | | | |
| Equity | $ 3,526,671,825 | $ 218,262,613 | $ 3,744,934,438 |
| **Total Liabilities and Equity** | $ 3,526,671,825 | $ 218,262,613 | $ 3,744,934,438 |
| | | | |
| **Receipts** | | | |
| Corporate Environmental | - | 3,137,141 | 3,137,141 |
| Cost Recoveries | - | 53,246,618 | 53,246,618 |
| Fines & Penalties | - | 3,451,837 | 3,451,837 |
| Total Revenue | - | 59,835,596 | 59,835,596 |
| Appropriations Received | - | 1,280,570,288 | 1,280,570,288 |
| Interest Income | - | 14,967,685 | 14,967,685 |
| **Total Receipts** | $ - | $ 1,355,373,569 | $ 1,355,373,569 |
| | | | |
| **Outlays** | | | |
| Transfers to/from EPA, Net | $ 1,308,704,084 | $ (1,308,704,084) | $ - |
| **Total Outlays** | 1,308,704,084 | (1,308,704,084) | - |
| **Net Income** | $ 1,308,704,084 | $ 46,669,485 | $ 1,355,373,569 |

In FY 2010, the EPA received an appropriation of $1.28 billion for Superfund. Treasury's Bureau of Public Debt (BPD), the manager of the Superfund Trust Fund assets, records a liability to EPA for the amount of the appropriation. BPD does this to indicate those trust fund assets that have been assigned for use and, therefore, are not available for appropriation. As of September 30, 2010 and 2009, the Treasury Trust Fund has a liability to EPA for previously appropriated funds of $3.53 billion and $3.28 billion, respectively.

| SUPERFUND FY 2009 | EPA | | Treasury | Combined |
|---|---|---|---|---|
| **Undistributed Balances** | | | | |
| Uninvested Fund Balance | $ - | $ | (7,975) $ | (7,975) |
| Total Undisbursed Balance | - | | (7,975) | (7,975) |
| Interest Receivable | - | | 19,624 | 19,624 |
| Investments, Net | 3,277,721 | | 159,991 | 3,437,712 |
| **Total Assets** | $ 3,277,721 | $ | 171,640 $ | 3,449,361 |
| **Liabilities & Equity** | | | | |
| Receipts and Outlays | - | | | - |
| Equity | $ 3,277,721 | $ | 171,640 $ | 3,449,361 |
| **Total Liabilities and Equity** | $ 3,277,721 | $ | 171,640 $ | 3,449,361 |
| **Receipts** | | | | |
| Cost Recoveries | $ - | $ | 96,782 $ | 96,782 |
| Fines & Penalties | - | | 1,374 | 1,374 |
| Total Revenue | - | | 98,156 | 98,156 |
| Appropriations Received | - | | 1,747,911 | 1,747,911 |
| Interest Income | - | | 52,064 | 52,064 |
| **Total Receipts** | $ - | $ | 1,898,131 $ | 1,898,131 |
| **Outlays** | | | | |
| Transfers to/from EPA, Net | $ 1,905,845 | $ | (1,905,845) $ | - |
| **Total Outlays** | 1,905,845 | | (1,905,845) | - |
| **Net Income** | $ **1,905,845** | $ | **(7,714)** $ | **1,898,131** |

# LUST

LUST is supported primarily by a sales tax on motor fuels to clean up LUST waste sites. In FY 2010 and 2009, there were no fund receipts from cost recoveries. The following represents the LUST Trust Fund as maintained by Treasury. The amounts contained in these notes are provided by Treasury. Outlays represent appropriations received by EPA's LUST Trust Fund; such funds are eliminated on consolidation with the LUST Trust Fund maintained by Treasury.

| LUST FY 2010 | EPA | Treasury | Combined |
|---|---|---|---|
| **Undistributed Balances** | | | |
| Uninvested Fund Balance | $          - | $    (5,349,000) | $    (5,349,000) |
| Total Undisbursed Balance | - | (5,349,000) | (5,349,000) |
| Interest Receivable | - | 20,815,275 | 20,815,275 |
| Investments, Net | 210,146,189 | 3,271,951,525 | 3,482,097,714 |
| **Total Assets** | $    210,146,189 | $    3,287,417,800 | $    3,497,563,989 |
| **Liabilities & Equity** | | | |
| **Equity** | $    210,146,189 | $    3,287,417,800 | $    3,497,563,989 |
| **Receipts** | | | |
| Highway TF Tax | $          - | $    158,254,000 | $    158,254,000 |
| Airport TF Tax | - | 10,685,000 | 10,685,000 |
| Inland TF Tax | - | 51,000 | 51,000 |
| Total Revenue | - | 168,990,000 | 168,990,000 |
| Interest Income | - | 115,523,147 | 115,523,147 |
| **Total Receipts** | $          - | $    284,513,147 | $    284,513,147 |
| **Outlays** | | | |
| Transfers to/from EPA, Net | $    103,901,000 | $    (103,901,000) | $          - |
| **Total Outlays** | 103,901,000 | (103,901,000) | - |
| **Net Income** | $    **103,901,000** | $    **180,612,147** | $    **284,513,147** |

| LUST FY 2009 | | | EPA | Treasury | Combined |
|---|---|---|---|---|---|
| **Undistributed Balances** | | | | | |
| Uninvested Fund Balance | $ | - | $ | (10,359) $ | (10,359) |
| Total Undisbursed Balance | | - | | (10,359) | (10,359) |
| Interest Receivable | | - | | 22,838 | 22,838 |
| Investments, Net | | 305,445 | | 3,094,325 | 3,399,770 |
| **Total Assets** | $ | 305,445 | $ | 3,106,804 $ | 3,412,249 |
| **Liabilities & Equity** | | | | | |
| **Equity** | $ | 305,445 | $ | 3,106,804 $ | 3,412,249 |
| | | | | | |
| **Receipts** | | | | | |
| Highway TF Tax | $ | - | $ | 159,719 $ | 159,719 |
| Airport TF Tax | | - | | 9,454 | 9,454 |
| Inland TF Tax | | - | | 13 | 13 |
| Total Revenue | | - | | 169,186 | 169,186 |
| Interest Income | | - | | 124,087 | 124,087 |
| **Total Receipts** | $ | - | $ | 293,273 $ | 293,273 |
| **Outlays** | | | | | |
| Transfers to/from EPA, Net | $ | 312,577 | $ | (312,577) $ | - |
| **Total Outlays** | | 312,577 | | (312,577) | - |
| **Net Income** | $ | **312,577** | $ | **(19,304)** $ | **293,273** |

## Note 39. Antideficiency Act Violation Reported in 2010

During FY 2004, EPA awarded a contract in the amount of $194 thousand for the analysis of drinking-water. The funding was available for FY 2004 and FY 2005. The contract performance period crossed three fiscal years, FY 2004, FY 2005, and FY 2006. As a result, the obligation of funds went beyond the appropriation resulting in an Antideficiency Act violation. On July 14, 2010 EPA transmitted, as required by OMB Circular A-11, Section 145, written notifications to the (1) President, (2) President of the Senate, (3) Speaker of the House of Representatives, (4) Comptroller General, and (5) the Director of OMB.

**Environmental Protection Agency**
**As of September 30, 2010**
**(Dollars in Thousands)**

## 1. Deferred Maintenance

Deferred maintenance is maintenance that was not performed when it should have been, that was scheduled and not performed, or that was delayed for a future period. Maintenance is the act of keeping property, plant, and equipment (PP&E) in acceptable operating condition and includes preventive maintenance, normal repairs, replacement of parts and structural components, and other activities needed to preserve the asset so that it can deliver acceptable performance and achieve its expected life. Maintenance excludes activities aimed at expanding the capacity of an asset or otherwise upgrading it to serve needs different from or significantly greater than those originally intended.

The EPA classifies tangible property, plant, and equipment as follows: (1) EPA-Held Equipment, (2) Contractor-Held Equipment, (3) Land and Buildings, and, (4) Capital Leases. The condition assessment survey method of measuring deferred maintenance is utilized. The Agency adopts requirements or standards for acceptable operating condition in conformance with industry practices. No deferred maintenance was reported for any of the four categories.

## 2. Stewardship Land

Stewardship land is acquired as contaminated sites in need of remediation and clean-up; thus the quality of the land is far-below the standard for usable and manageable land. Easements on stewardship lands are in good and usable condition but acquired in order to gain access to contaminated sites.

# Environmental Protection Agency
## As of September 30, 2010
### (Dollars in Thousands)

## 3. Supplemental Combined Statement of Budgetary Resources For the Period Ending September 30, 2010

| BUDGETARY RESOURCE | EPM | FIFRA | LUST | S&T | STAG | OTHER | TOTAL |
|---|---|---|---|---|---|---|---|
| Unobligated Balance Brought Forward, October 1 | $ 596,033 $ | 4,163 $ | 13,113 $ | 230,607 $ | 1,135,800 $ | 1,723,306 $ | 3,703,022 |
| Recoveries of prior year unpaid obligations | 32,763 | | 7,137 | 5,155 | 55,779 | 176,938 | 277,771 |
| Budgetary Authority: | | | | | | | |
| Appropriation | 2,993,779 | | - | 848,049 | 4,978,223 | 1,436,115 | 10,256,166 |
| Borrowing Authority | | | | | | 52 | 52 |
| Spending Authority from Offsetting Collections: | | | | | | | |
| Collected | 98,534 | 23,237 | 36 | 12,260 | 4,719 | 780,000 | 918,786 |
| Change in receivables from Federal sources | (2,786) | - | | (116) | - | 1,157 | (1,746) |
| Advance received | (6,687) | (1,151) | - | (5,677) | | 248,074 | 234,559 |
| Without advance from Federal source | (174,170) | - | | (947) | - | 42,629 | (132,489) |
| Expenditure Transfers from trust funds | - | | | 26,834 | | 9,975 | 36,809 |
| Nonexpenditure transers, net anticipated and actual | (9,070) | | 113,101 | - | (7,930) | 1,273,244 | 1,369,345 |
| Temporarily not available pursuant to Public Law | | | (9,200) | | | (2,600) | (11,800) |
| Permanently not available | (17,715) | | | (7,137) | (38,796) | (9,806) | (73,453) |
| Total Budgetary Resources | $ 3,510,680 $ | 26,249 $ | 124,186 $ | 1,109,028 $ | 6,127,795 $ | 5,679,083 $ | 16,577,022 |
| | | | | | | | |
| STATUS OF BUDGETARY RESOURCES | | | | | | | |
| Obligations Incurred: | | | | | | | |
| Direct | $ 2,996,093 $ | - $ | 117,024 $ | 846,166 $ | 4,410,501 $ | 2,890,669 $ | 11,260,452 |
| Reimbursable | 33,158 | 24,473 | - | 9,663 | - | 622,935 | 690,229 |
| Total Obligations Incurred | 3,029,250 | 24,473 | 117,024 | 855,829 | 4,410,501 | 3,513,604 | 11,950,681 |
| Unobligated Balances: | | | | | | | |
| Unobligated funds apportioned | 342,894 | 1,776 | 7,058 | 202,007 | 1,717,294 | 2,159,783 | 4,430,813 |
| Unobligated balance not available | 138,536 | 0 | 105 | 51,191 | (0) | 5,697 | 195,528 |
| Total Status of Budgetary Resources | $ 3,510,680 $ | 26,249 $ | 124,186 $ | 1,109,028 $ | 6,127,795 $ | 5,679,083 $ | 16,577,022 |
| | | | | | | | |
| CHANGE IN OBLIGATED BALANCE | | | | | | | |
| Obligated Balance, Net | | | | | | | |
| Unpaid obligations brought forward, October 1 | $ 878,039 $ | 2,990 $ | 327,859 $ | 423,294 $ | 12,136,931 $ | 2,019,276 $ | 15,788,389 |
| Less: Uncollected customer payments from Federal sources brought forward, October 1 | (333,906) | - | | (36,245) | - | (203,673) | (573,824) |
| Total unpaid obligation balance, net | 544,133 | 2,990 | 327,859 | 387,048 | 12,136,931 | 1,815,603 | 15,214,565 |
| Obligations incurred net | 3,029,250 | 24,473 | 117,024 | 855,829 | 4,410,501 | 3,513,604 | 11,950,681 |
| Less: Gross outlays | (2,655,567) | (25,036) | (174,282) | (862,403) | (6,410,218) | (3,460,886) | (13,588,391) |
| Less: Recoveries of prior year unpaid obligations, actual | (32,763) | | (7,137) | (5,155) | (55,779) | (176,938) | (277,771) |
| Change in uncollected customer payments from Federal sources | 176,957 | - | | 1,181 | - | (44,268) | 133,869 |
| Total | 1,062,011 | 2,427 | 263,464 | 376,500 | 10,081,435 | 1,647,114 | 13,432,953 |
| | | | | | | | |
| Obligated Balance, net, end of period: | | | | | | | |
| Unpaid obligations | 1,218,961 | 2,427 | 263,464 | 411,565 | 10,081,435 | 1,895,056 | 13,872,909 |
| Less: Uncollected customer payments from Federal sources | (156,949) | - | | (35,065) | - | (247,942) | (439,956) |
| Total, unpaid obligated balance, net, end of period | $ 1,062,012 $ | 2,427 $ | 263,464 $ | 376,500 $ | 10,081,435 $ | 1,647,114 $ | 13,432,953 |
| | | | | | | | |
| NET OUTLAYS | | | | | | | |
| Gross outlays | $ 2,655,567 $ | 25,036 $ | 174,282 $ | 862,403 $ | 6,410,218 $ | 3,460,886 $ | 13,588,391 |
| Less: Offsetting collections | (91,847) | (22,086) | (36) | (33,534) | (4,719) | (1,037,566) | (1,189,788) |
| Less: Distributed Offsetting Receipts | | | | | | (1,402,960) | (1,402,960) |
| Total, Net Outlays | $ 2,563,720 $ | 2,950 $ | 174,247 $ | 828,869 $ | 6,405,499 $ | 1,020,359 $ | 10,995,643 |

**Environmental Protection Agency**
**Required Supplemental Stewardship Information**
**For the Year Ended September 30, 2010**
**(Dollars in Thousands)**

*INVESTMENT IN THE NATION'S RESEARCH AND DEVELOPMENT:*

EPA's Office of Research and Development provides the scientific basis for EPA decision-making by conducting cutting-edge science and technical analysis to assist in the development of sustainable solutions to our environmental problems and more innovative and effective approaches to reducing environmental risks. EPA is unique among scientific institutions in combining research, analysis, and the integration of scientific information across the full spectrum of health and ecological issues and across the risk assessment and risk management paradigm. Research enables us to assess and identify the most important sources of risk to human health and the environment and by so doing, informs our priority-setting, ensures credibility for our policies, and guides our deployment of resources.

Among the Agency's highest priorities are research programs that address: the development of alternative techniques for prioritizing chemicals for further testing through computational toxicology; the environmental effects on children's health; the potential risks and effects of manufactured nanomaterials on human health and the environment; the impacts of global change and providing information to policy makers to help them adapt to a changing climate; the potential risks of unregulated contaminants in drinking water; the development of recreational water quality criteria; the health effects of air pollutants such as particulate matter; the protection of the nation's ecosystems; and the provision of near-term, appropriate, affordable, reliable, tested, and effective technologies and guidance for potential threats to homeland security. EPA also supports regulatory decision-making with chemical risk assessments.

For FY 2010, the full cost of the Agency's Research and Development activities totaled over $663M. Below is a breakout of the expenses (dollars in thousands):

|  | FY 2006 | FY2007 | FY2008 | FY2009 | FY2010 |
|---|---|---|---|---|---|
| Programmatic Expenses | $630,438 | $624,088 | $597,080 | $600,552 | $590,790 |
| Allocated Expenses | $104,167 | $100,553 | $103,773 | $119,630 | $71,958 |

Each of EPA's strategic goals has a Science and Research Objective.

*INVESTMENT IN THE NATION'S INFRASTRUCTURE:*

The Agency makes significant investments in the nation's drinking water and clean water infrastructure. The investments are the result of three programs: the Construction Grants Program which is being phased out and two State Revolving Fund (SRF) programs.

Construction Grants Program: During the 1970s and 1980s, the Construction Grants Program was a source of Federal funds, providing more than $60 billion of direct grants for the construction of public wastewater treatment projects. These projects, which constituted a significant contribution to the nation's water infrastructure, included sewage treatment plants, pumping stations, and collection and intercept sewers, rehabilitation of sewer systems, and the control of combined sewer overflows. The construction grants led to the improvement of water quality in thousands of municipalities nationwide.

Congress set 1990 as the last year that funds would be appropriated for Construction Grants. Projects funded in 1990 and prior will continue until completion. After 1990, EPA shifted the focus of municipal financial assistance from grants to loans that are provided by State Revolving Funds.

State Revolving Funds: EPA provides capital, in the form of capitalization grants, to state revolving funds which state governments use to make loans to individuals, businesses, and governmental entities for the construction of wastewater and drinking water treatment infrastructure. When the loans are repaid to the state revolving fund, the collections are used to finance new loans for new construction projects. The capital is reused by the states and is not returned to the Federal Government.

The Agency also is appropriated funds to finance the construction of infrastructure outside the Revolving Funds. These are reported below as Other Infrastructure Grants.

The Agency's expenses related to investments in the nation's Water Infrastructure are outlined below (dollars in thousands):

|  | FY 2006 | FY 2007 | FY 2008 | FY 2009 | FY 2010 |
|---|---|---|---|---|---|
| Construction Grants | $39,193 | $9,975 | $11,517 | $30,950 | $13,009 |
| Clean Water SRF | $1,339,702 | $1,399,616 | $1,063,825 | $835,446 | $679,332 |
| Safe Drinking Water SRF | $910,032 | $962,903 | $816,038 | $906,803 | $733,804 |
| Other Infrastructure Grants | $411,023 | $381,481 | $388,555 | $306,366 | $229,632 |
| Allocated Expenses | $446,113 | $443,716 | $396,253 | $414,249 | $201,674 |

## HUMAN CAPITAL

Agencies are required to report expenses incurred to train the public with the intent of increasing or maintaining the nation's economic productive capacity. Training, public awareness, and research fellowships are components of many of the Agency's programs and are effective in achieving the Agency's mission of protecting public health and the environment, but the focus is on enhancing the nation's environmental, not economic, capacity.

The Agency's expenses related to investments in the Human Capital are outlined below (dollars in thousands):

|                              | FY 2006  | FY 2007  | FY 2008  | FY 2009  | FY 2010  |
| ---------------------------- | -------- | -------- | -------- | -------- | -------- |
| Training and Awareness Grants | $43,765  | $32,845  | $30,768  | $37,981  | $25,714  |
| Fellowships                  | $12,639  | $12,185  | $9,650   | $6,818   | $6,905   |
| Allocated Expenses           | $9,320   | $7,255   | $7,025   | $8,924   | $3,973   |

# Environmental Protection Agency
## Supplemental Information and Other Reporting Requirements
## Balance Sheet for Superfund Trust Fund
## For the Periods Ending September 30, 2010 and 2009
### (Dollars in Thousands)
### (Unaudited)

|  | FY 2010 | FY 2009 |
|---|---:|---:|
| **ASSETS** | | |
| Intragovernmental: | | |
| Fund Balance With Treasury (Note S1) | $ 106,247 | $ 62,631 |
| Investments | 3,740,700 | 3,457,338 |
| Accounts Receivable, Net | 27,323 | 20,694 |
| Other | 12,941 | 23,100 |
| Total Intragovernmental | $ 3,887,211 | $ 3,563,763 |
| | | |
| Accounts Receivable, Net | 364,065 | 748,838 |
| Property, Plant & Equipment, Net | 101,714 | 81,216 |
| Other | 1,075 | 419 |
| **Total Assets** | $ **4,354,065** | $ **4,394,236** |
| | | |
| | | |
| **LIABILITIES** | | |
| Intragovernmental: | | |
| Accounts Payable and Accrued Liabilities | 45,641 | 47,787 |
| Custodial Liability | - | 187 |
| Other | 62,260 | 76,051 |
| Total Intragovernmental | $ 107,901 | $ 124,025 |
| | | |
| Accounts Payable & Accrued Liabilities | $ 178,045 | $ 183,477 |
| Pensions & Other Actuarial Liabilities | 6,420 | 7,829 |
| Cashout Advances, Superfund (Note S2) | 636,673 | 572,412 |
| Payroll & Benefits Payable | 45,792 | 44,604 |
| Other | 38,736 | 45,353 |
| Total Liabilities | $ 1,013,566 | $ 977,700 |
| | | |
| **NET POSITION** | | |
| Cumulative Results of Operations | 3,340,498 | 3,416,536 |
| Total Net Position | 3,340,498 | 3,416,536 |
| | | |
| **Total Liabilities and Net Position** | $ **4,354,065** | $ **4,394,236** |

**The accompanying notes are an integral part of these financial statements.**

# Environmental Protection Agency
## Supplemental Information and Other Reporting Requirements
## Statement of Net Cost for Superfund Trust Fund
## For the Periods Ending September 30, 2010 and 2009
### (Dollars in Thousands)
### (Unaudited)

|  | FY 2010 | FY 2009 |
|---|---|---|
| **COSTS** | | |
| Gross Costs | $ 1,844,712 | $ 1,672,246 |
| Expenses from Other Appropriations | 30,349 | 130,931 |
| Total Costs | 1,875,061 | 1,803,177 |
| Less: | | |
| Earned Revenue | 484,165 | 615,577 |
| **NET COST OF OPERATIONS** | $ 1,390,896 | $ 1,187,600 |

**The accompanying notes are an integral part of these financial statements.**

# Environmental Protection Agency
## Supplemental Information and Other Reporting Requirements
## Statement of Changes in Net Position for Superfund Trust Fund
## For the Periods Ending September 30, 2010 and 2009
### (Dollars in Thousands)
### (Unaudited)

|  |  | FY 2010 Earmarked Funds | | FY 2009 Earmarked Funds |
|---|---|---|---|---|
| **Cumulative Results of Operations:** |  |  |  |  |
|  |  |  |  |  |
| **Net Position - Beginning of Period** |  | 3,416,536 |  | 2,702,763 |
| Beginning Balances, as Adjusted | $ | 3,416,536 | $ | 2,702,763 |
|  |  |  |  |  |
| **Budgetary Financing Sources:** |  |  |  |  |
| Nonexchange Revenue - Securities Investment |  | 14,968 |  | 52,065 |
| Nonexchange Revenue - Other |  | 3,396 |  | (1,479) |
| Transfers In/Out |  | (39,168) |  | (54,393) |
| Trust Fund Appropriations |  | 1,280,570 |  | 1,747,911 |
| Income from Other Appropriations |  | 30,349 |  | 130,931 |
| Total Budgetary Financing Sources | $ | 1,290,115 | $ | 1,875,035 |
|  |  |  |  |  |
| **Other Financing Sources (Non-Exchange)** |  |  |  |  |
| Transfers In/Out |  | - |  | (84) |
| Imputed Financing Sources |  | 24,743 |  | 26,422 |
| Total Other Financing Sources | $ | 24,743 | $ | 26,338 |
|  |  |  |  |  |
| Net Cost of Operations |  | (1,390,896) |  | (1,187,600) |
|  |  |  |  |  |
| Net Change |  | (76,038) |  | 713,773 |
|  |  |  |  |  |
| **Cumulative Results of Operations** | $ | **3,340,498** | $ | **3,416,536** |

**The accompanying notes are an integral part of these financial statements.**

# Environmental Protection Agency
## Supplemental Information and Other Reporting Requirements
## Statement of Budgetary Resources for Superfund Trust Fund
## For the Periods Ending September 30, 2010 and 2009
### (Dollars in Thousands)
### (Unaudited)

| | FY 2010 | FY 2009 |
|---|---:|---:|
| **BUDGETARY RESOURCES** | | |
| Unobligated Balance, Brought Forward, October 1: | $ 1,605,363 | $ 1,513,176 |
| Adjusted Subtotal | 1,605,363 | 1,513,176 |
| Recoveries of Prior Year Unpaid Obligations | 171,423 | 118,278 |
| Budgetary Authority: | | |
| Appropriation | 36,809 | 636,392 |
| Borrowing Authority | - | - |
| Spending Authority from Offsetting Collections | | |
| Earned: | | |
| Collected | 518,936 | 292,403 |
| Change in Receivables from Federal Sources | 47 | 1,401 |
| Change in Unfilled Customer Orders: | | |
| Advance Received | 244,146 | 12,032 |
| Without Advance from Federal Sources | 4,423 | 4,574 |
| Anticipated for Rest of Year, Without Advances | - | - |
| Previously Unavailable | - | - |
| Expenditure Transfers from Trust Funds | - | - |
| Total Spending Authority from Offsetting Collections | 767,552 | 310,410 |
| Nonexpenditure Transfers, Net, Anticipated and Actual | 1,273,244 | 1,269,453 |
| Temporarily Not Available Pursuant to Public Law | (2,600) | - |
| Permanently Not Available | (4,102) | - |
| **Total Budgetary Resources** | $ 3,847,690 | $ 3,847,709 |
| | | |
| **STATUS OF BUDGETARY RESOURCES** | | |
| Obligations Incurred: | | |
| Direct | $ 1,475,861 | $ 1,996,048 |
| Reimbursable | 312,141 | 246,297 |
| Total Obligations Incurred | 1,788,002 | 2,242,345 |
| Unobligated Balances: | | |
| Apportioned | 2,058,813 | 1,593,443 |
| Exempt from Apportionment | - | - |
| Total Unobligated Balances | 2,058,813 | 1,593,443 |
| Unobligated Balances Not Available | 874 | 11,921 |
| **Total Status of Budgetary Resources (Note S6)** | $ 3,847,690 | $ 3,847,709 |

**The accompanying notes are an integral part of these financial statements.**

# Environmental Protection Agency
## Supplemental Information and Other Reporting Requirements
## Statement of Budgetary Resources for Superfund Trust Fund
## For the Periods Ending September 30, 2010 and 2009
### (Dollars in Thousands)
### (Unaudited)

|  | FY 2010 | FY 2009 |
|---|---|---|
| **CHANGE IN OBLIGATED BALANCE** | | |
| Obligated Balance, Net: | | |
| Unpaid Obligations, Brought Forward, October 1 | $ 1,861,908 | $ 1,392,311 |
| Adjusted Total | 1,861,908 | 1,392,311 |
| Less: Uncollected Customer Payments from Federal Sources, | | |
| Brought Forward, October 1 | (118,896) | (112,921) |
| Total Unpaid Obligated Balance, Net | 1,743,012 | 1,279,390 |
| Obligations Incurred, Net | 1,788,002 | 2,242,345 |
| Less: Gross Outlays | (1,785,572) | (1,654,470) |
| Obligated Balance Transferred, Net: | | |
| Actual Transfers, Unpaid Obligations | - | - |
| Actual Transfers, Uncollected Customer Payments from Federal | - | - |
| Total Unpaid Obligated Balance Transferred, Net | - | - |
| Less: Recoveries of Prior Year Unpaid Obligations, Actual | (171,423) | (118,278) |
| Change in Uncollected Customer Payments from Federal Sources | (4,471) | (5,975) |
| Total, Change in Obligated Balance | 1,569,549 | 1,743,012 |
| | | |
| Obligated Balance, Net, End of Period: | | |
| Unpaid Obligations | 1,692,915 | 1,861,908 |
| Less: Uncollected Customer Payments from Federal Sources | (123,366) | (118,896) |
| Total, Unpaid Obligated Balance, Net, End of Period | $ 1,569,549 | $ 1,743,012 |
| | | |
| | | |
| **NET OUTLAYS** | | |
| Net Outlays: | | |
| Gross Outlays (Note S6) | $ 1,785,572 | $ 1,654,470 |
| Less: Offsetting Collections (Note S6) | (763,081) | (304,434) |
| Less: Distributed Offsetting Receipts* (Note S6) | (53,247) | (1,244,694) |
| **Total, Net Outlays** | $ 969,244 | $ 105,342 |

Offsetting receipts line includes the amount in 68X0250 (payment to trust fund) from Treasury

The payment cannot be made directly through the trust fund, but must go through a "pass-through" fund

**The accompanying notes are an integral part of these financial statements.**

# Environmental Protection Agency
## Supplemental Information and Other Reporting Requirements
## Related Notes to Superfund Trust Financial Statements
## For the Periods Ending September 30, 2010 and 2009
### (Dollars in Thousands)
### (Unaudited)

---

### *Note S1. Fund Balance with Treasury for Superfund Trust*

Fund Balances with Treasury for the Superfund as of September 30, 2010 and 2009 is $106.2 million and $62.63 million, respectively. Fund balances are available to pay current liabilities and to finance authorized purchase commitments (see Status of Fund Balances below).

| Status of Fund Balances: | | FY 2010 | | FY 2009 |
|---|---|---|---|---|
| Unobligated Amounts in Fund Balance: | | | | |
| Available for Obligation | $ | 2,058,813 | $ | 1,593,443 |
| Unavailable for Obligation | | 874 | | 11,824 |
| Net Receivables from Invested Balances | | (3,526,672) | | (3,277,674) |
| Balances in Treasury Trust Fund | | (1,115) | | (7,975) |
| Obligated Balance not yet Disbursed | | 1,574,347 | | 1,743,013 |
| **Totals** | $ | **106,247** | $ | **62,631** |

The funds available for obligation may be apportioned by the OMB for new obligations at the beginning of the following fiscal year. Funds unavailable for obligation are mostly balances in expired funds, which are available only for adjustments of existing obligations.

---

### *Note S2. Cashout Advances, Superfund*

Cashout Advances are funds received by EPA, a state, or another PRP under the terms of a settlement agreement (e.g., consent decree) to finance response action costs at a specified Superfund site. Under CERCLA Section 122(b)(3), cashout funds received by EPA are placed in site-specific, interest bearing accounts known as special accounts and are used for potential future work at such sites in accordance with the terms of the settlement agreement. Funds placed in special accounts may be disbursed to PRPs, to states that take responsibility for the site, or to other Federal agencies to conduct or finance response actions in lieu of EPA without further appropriation by Congress. As of September 30, 2010 and 2009, cashout advances are $637 million and $572 million.

## Note S3. Superfund State Credits

Authorizing statutory language for Superfund and related Federal regulations require states to enter into SSCs when EPA assumes the lead for a remedial action in their state. The SSC defines the state's role in the remedial action and obtains the state's assurance that they will share in the cost of the remedial action. Under Superfund's authorizing statutory language, states will provide EPA with a 10 percent cost share for remedial action costs incurred at privately owned or operated sites, and at least 50 percent of all response activities (i.e., removal, remedial planning, remedial action, and enforcement) at publicly operated sites. In some cases, states may use EPA approved credits to reduce all or part of their cost share requirement that would otherwise be borne by the states. Credit is limited to state site-specific expenses EPA has determined to be reasonable, documented, direct out-of-pocket expenditures of non-Federal funds for remedial action.

Once EPA has reviewed and approved a state's claim for credit, the state must first apply the credit at the site where it was earned. The state may apply any excess/remaining credit to another site when approved by EPA. As of September 30, 2010, the total remaining state credits have been estimated at $20.9 million. The estimated ending credit balance on September 30, 2009 was $21.9 million.

## Note S4. Superfund Preauthorized Mixed Funding Agreements

Under Superfund preauthorized mixed funding agreements, PRPs agree to perform response actions at their sites with the understanding that EPA will reimburse them a certain percentage of their total response action costs. EPA's authority to enter into mixed funding agreements is provided under CERCLA Section 111(a)(2). Under CERCLA Section 122(b)(1), as amended by SARA, PRPs may assert a claim against the Superfund Trust Fund for a portion of the costs they incurred while conducting a preauthorized response action agreed to under a mixed funding agreement. As of September 30, 2010, EPA had 6 outstanding preauthorized mixed funding agreements with obligations totaling $15.6 million. As of September 30, 2009, EPA had 9 for $19.9 million. A liability is not recognized for these amounts until all work has been performed by the PRP and has been approved by EPA for payment. Further, EPA will not disburse any funds under these agreements until the PRP's application, claim, and claims adjustment processes have been reviewed and approved by EPA.

## Note S5. Income and Expenses from other Appropriations; General Support Services Charged to Superfund

The Statement of Net Cost reports costs that represent the full costs of the program outputs. These costs consist of the direct costs and all other costs that can be directly traced, assigned on a cause and effect basis, or reasonably allocated to program outputs.

During FYs 2010 and 2009, the EPM appropriation funded a variety of programmatic and non-programmatic activities across the Agency, subject to statutory requirements. This appropriation was created to fund personnel compensation and benefits, travel, procurement, and contract activities. This distribution is calculated using a combination of specific identification of expenses to Reporting Entities, and a weighted average that distributes expenses proportionately to total programmatic expenses. As illustrated below, this estimate does not impact the consolidated totals of the Statement of Net Cost or the Statement of Changes in Net Position.

| | FY 2010 | | | FY 2009 | | |
|---|---|---|---|---|---|---|
| | Income from Other Appropriations | Expenses from Other Appropriations | Net Effect | Income from Other Appropriations | Expenses from Other Appropriations | Net Effect |
| Superfund | $ 30,349 | (30,349) | $ - | $ 130,931 | (130,931) | $ - |
| All Others | (30,349) | 30,349 | - | (130,931) | 130,931 | - |
| Total | $ - | $ - | $ - | $ - | $ - | $ - |

In addition, the related general support services costs allocated to the Superfund Trust Fund from the S&T and EPM funds are $194 thousand for FY 2010 and $234 thousand for FY 2009.

---

## Note S6. Reconciliation of the Statement of Budgetary Resources to the President's Budget

Budgetary resources, obligations incurred, and outlays, as presented in the audited FY 2009 Statement of Budgetary Resources, will be reconciled to the amounts included in the Budget of the United States Government when they become available. The Budget of the United States Government with actual numbers for FY 2010 has not yet been published. We expect it will be published by March 2011, and it will be available on the OMB website at http://www.whitehouse.gov/omb/budget/fy20101. The actual amounts published for the year ended September 30, 2009 are included in EPA's FY 2009 financial statement disclosures.

| FY 2009 | Budgetary Resources | Obligations | Offsetting Receipts | Net Outlays |
|---|---|---|---|---|
| Statement of Budgetary Resources | $ 3,847,709 | $ 2,242,345 | $ 1,244,694 | $ 1,350,036 |
| Rounding Differences** | (709) | (345) | (694) | (36) |
| Reported in Budget of the U. S. Government | $ 3,847,000 | $ 2,242,000 | $ 1,244,000 | $ 1,350,000 |

* Balances are rounded to millions in the Budget Appendix.

## Note S7. *Superfund Eliminations*

The Superfund Trust Fund has intra-agency activities with other EPA funds which are eliminated on the consolidated Balance Sheet and the Statement of Net Cost. These are listed below:

|  | FY 2010 | FY 2009 |
|---|---|---|
| Advances | $9,265 | $14,327 |
| Expenditure Transfers Payable | $25,555 | $25,189 |
| Accrued Liabilities | $2,214 | $2,991 |
| Expenses | $33,419 | $29,100 |
| Transfers | $38,016 | $54,392 |

# Agency's Response to Draft Report

**November 09, 2010**

**MEMORANDUM**

**SUBJECT**:    Audit of EPA's Fiscal 2010 and 2009 Consolidated Financial Statements

**FROM**:       Barbara J. Bennett /s/
              Chief Financial    fficerO

**TO**:         Arthur A. Elkins, Jr.
              Inspector General

Fiscal Year 2010 marks another successful financial statements audit cycle for the U.S. Environmental Protection Agency. This year, we broadened Agency partnerships with a focus on strengthening fiscal integrity, enhancing core business operations, and contributing to Agency-wide performance management systems. We are proud of the many accomplishments and thank you for identifying additional areas for improvement in the draft Inspector General's Audit Report. The audit work performed will help shape future financial management initiatives.

Our offices worked together to expand stakeholder involvement, thereby engaging all parts of the Agency in fiscal stewardship yielding significant results. Attached are the Agency's responses to this audit report. Detailed corrective action plans will be provided to you and your staff within 90-days of the issuance of the final audit report. Please let me know if you have any questions, or your staff can contact Stefan Silzer, Acting Director, Office of Financial Management of 202-564-5389 regarding the audit.

Attachment

cc: Mark Bialek, Deputy Inspector General
Craig E. Hooks, Assistant Administrator, Office of Administration and Resources Management
Malcolm D. Jackson, Assistant Administrator, Office of Environmental Information
Maryann Froehlich, Deputy Chief Financial Officer
Melissa Heist, Assistant Inspector General
Joshua Baylson, Associate Chief Financial Officer
Stefan Silzer, Acting Director, Office of Financial Management
Raffael Stein, Director, Office of Financial Services
Paul Curtis, Director Financial Statements Audit
Jim Wood, Director, Cincinnati Finance Center
Stella Whitsell, Staff Director, Reporting and Analysis Staff
Jeanne Conklin, Staff Director, Financial Policy and Planning Staff

**Attachment 1**

**Response to Draft Audit of EPA's Fiscal 2010 and 2009 Consolidated Financial Statements**

**1 - Further Improvements Needed in Reviewing the Superfund State Contract (SSC) Unearned Revenue Spreadsheets**

**Recommendations**

We recommend that the Office of the Chief Financial Officer (OCFO):

1. Work with the regions to review prior years' fund code "T" disbursements data on the SSC spreadsheets.

**Response: (Concur)**

Office of Financial Service (OFS) will work with the regions during the close out and reconciliation process described in recommendation 3 (of this Position Paper) and make necessary adjustments as a result of the regional review.

2. Work with the regions to review the spreadsheet data for the estimated site costs, state cost share, credits, and billings.

**Response: (Concur)**

OFS has reviewed and reconciled the site billing and disbursement data presented on the accrual spreadsheets as of the fourth quarter of fiscal 2010 and appropriate adjustments were made based on our review as well as additional issues identified by auditors. In fiscal 2011, OFS will continue to work with the regions to ensure the estimated site costs, state cost share, and credits are correctly reported on the accrual spreadsheets. OFS has made progress in this area working directly with some regions to ensure they understand how and when the data needs to be updated on the accrual spreadsheets for credits and state cost share. OFS will continue this effort with the remaining regions during fiscal 2011. In addition, OFS will request that the percentage of sites reviewed for regional A-123 SSC process be increased for the fiscal 2011 review.

3. Require regions to report to Cincinnati Finance Center (CFC) the SSC site closeout amounts, including the final actual site costs separated by "T" and "TR1" disbursements, final state share, and the amount of refund paid or final billing.

**Response: (Concur)**

OFS will continue its efforts to request the regions to complete the close out process for SSC sites that are listed as "closed" on the accrual spreadsheets. OFS will remind the regions quarterly to work on the "closed" sites and complete all financial and/or administrative actions that are needed. As part of the close out process, regions will be confirming and/or adjusting various data on the accrual spreadsheets which will include the fund code 'T' and "TR1" disbursements.

4. Review the quarterly SSC spreadsheets to determine whether the site data are reasonable and the resulting site calculations are logical. Specifically, review the data for billings, credits, or unearned revenue in excess of state cost shares; no estimated site costs; no billings; reimbursable "TR1" expenses in excess of billings; and closed sites with accrued unbilled costs or unearned revenue.

**Response: (Concur)**

OFS will include additional reviews on the SSC accrual spreadsheets to address the potential concerns described in the Office of Inspector General (OIG) recommendations. These procedures will be included as part of the fiscal 2011 SSC accrual process.


## 2- EPA Should Assess Collectability of Receivables and Record Any Needed Allowances for Doubtful Accounts.

### Recommendations

We recommend that the Office of the Chief Financial Officer require the Office of Financial Services to:

5. Establish a federal allowance for $6.6 million, which remains on the Twin Cities site receivable.

**Response: (Non-Concur)**

OCFO has determined that the full $12.9 Million is collectable in accordance with Statement of Federal Financial Accounting Standards Number 1, Accounting for Selected Assets and Liabilities. We have based our determination on the fact that the Department of Defense is seeking appropriated funds to partially cover their liability and has booked a $12.9 Million liability. Therefore, EPA deems the entire $12.9 million receivable to be collectable.

| Your Agency | 68 | Select | | Trading Partner | 68 | |
|---|---|---|---|---|---|---|
| Trading Partner | 21 | Select | | Your Agency | 21 | |
| Recip Category | 22 | Select | | Category | 22 | |

| Your Agency Data | | | | Your Partner's Data | | | |
|---|---|---|---|---|---|---|---|
| Fund | FundTitle | SGL | Total | Fund | FundTitle | SGL | Total |
| 68008145 | HAZARDOUS SUBSTANCE SUPERFUND | 1310 | 13,021,672 | 21000021 | ALL ARMY FUNDS | 1310 | 66,424 |
| 68005555 | UNAVAILABLE RECEIPTS ACCOUNTS | 1310 | 37,601 | | | 2110 | 13,059,273 |
| Grand Total | | | 13,059,273 | Grand Total | | | 13,125,697 |

6. Review collectability of open federal accounts receivables and establish an allowance and/or write-off.

**Response: (Concur)**

CFC will review remaining open federal account receivables to ensure accurate status is reflected and reconcilable to the general ledger.

7. Establish procedures to ensure that CFC timely bills federal agencies within their authorized appropriation period.

**Response: (Concur)**

Procedures are in place to ensure the Finance Centers bill federal agencies within the authorized appropriation period. Environmental Protection Agency (EPA) Resource Management Directives System (RMDS) 2540-12, Intra-governmental Business Rules, http://intranet.epa.gov/ocfo/policies/direct/2540-12.pdf sets forth the Agency-wide financial policy for intra-governmental business rules. The policy states that intra-governmental business transactions will be processed, reconciled, and resolved in accordance with Treasury Financial Manual (TFM) Bulletin No. 2007-03 Section VI, Procurement Requirements, http://www.fms.treas.gov/tfm/vol1/07-03.pdf. The TFM Bulletin establishes that the agreement/order shall include"… (d) the effective date and duration of the agreement, to include the expiration of the funding source, (e) the amount and the method of payment, and (f) the method and frequency of performance (revenue and expenses) reporting:".

## 3 – Improvements Needed In Controls for Headquarters Personal Property

We recommend that the Assistant Administrator for Administration and Resources Management require the Director, Facilities Management and Services Division, (FMSD) to:

**Recommendations**

8. Develop a management-level property management training course and require completion of the course by all EPA managers.

   **Response: (Concur)**

   FMSD is working to develop a mandatory, annual, on-line training course for all employees with special emphasis on roles and responsibilities of managers and supervisors. The course will provide vital information on property policy and procedures and provide notice to all employees regarding the potential for personal liability for property assigned to them. Course development will be completed in February 2011.

9. Adequately address and resolve the issue and determine why personal property items are missing.

**Response: (Concur; additional information provided)**

To establish some background, it should be noted that the personal property inventory process was disrupted during FY 2009 as a result of implementation of the Customer Technology Solutions (CTS) computer replacement project. The Headquarters' inventory conducted from January through May, 2010, presented the first opportunity to thoroughly review the impact of the CTS project on the property inventory. Unfortunately, the results of the inventory indicated that there were 2,272 items unaccounted for, with an original purchase value of $6.3 million.

OARM took immediate steps to locate the missing items, and with the assistance and cooperation of Office of Environmental Information, has found 1,222 items or 54% of the outstanding items leaving 1,050 items remaining. As a result, the original purchase value at risk was reduced by $4 million or 64% to the current total of $2.2 million. OARM's efforts are continuing, and it is anticipated that most of the outstanding items will be located over the coming weeks, especially during the ongoing spot inventories.

Additional specific actions include: multiple re-inventories involving those custodial areas having missing items; re-inventories of numerous storage areas including those where CTS equipment has been stored; and collaboration with OEI on a separate inventory which is planned for completion in December.

OARM is continuing focused spot inventories which are expected to locate additional items and will begin the comprehensive FY2011 annual inventory process in January 2011. This effort will enable OARM to identify items that are unaccounted for as well as new items added to the inventory between October and January.

OARM has requested that the Headquarters Board of Survey (BOS) delay its review of items unaccounted for in FY 2010 for three months (October – January). The BOS is comprised of five employees from several Headquarters Program Offices and convenes at the end of each fiscal year to resolve missing property issues. This additional time will enable OARM to continue efforts to locate as many items as possible.

While the CTS project was a major factor, there were several additional factors which contributed to the unaccountable personal property at Headquarters. OARM is taking actions to address each of these factors and strengthen the integrity of the property management process. Key factors include:

a. A need for increased awareness among employees of property policy and practices. Property is frequently purchased, shipped, relocated, disposed of or otherwise reassigned without attention to the procedure or necessary documentation required.

b.  Custodial Officers are assigned property responsibilities as collateral duties and are generally not in a position to enforce compliance.

c.  Many of the missing items are cell phones and blackberries which are frequently provided absent proper tracking protocol.

d.  Property is currently tracked by location and not by the individual. This inability to associate individual responsibility with assigned property has led to a lack of accountability for personal property.

Consistent with its previous commitment, OARM is providing the rigorous management oversight that is required to meet and avoid the current challenges. The first priority action taken was to reassign responsibility for the Personal Property program to the Deputy Division Director to ensure the necessary level of attention. Further, additional resources have been dedicated to support program operations. Third, training will be required for all employees. By taking these and other corrective actions, OARM is confident that it will continue to strengthen the necessary oversight and control of Headquarters' personal property and minimize risks associated with the program.

## 4 – EPA Should Continue Efforts to Reconcile Intra-governmental Transactions

## Recommendation

We recommend that the Office of the Chief Financial Officer:

10. Continue efforts to reconcile EPA's intra-governmental transactions and make appropriate adjustments to comply with federal financial reporting requirements.

**Response: (Concur with recommended change to wording)**

OFS will continue to reconcile its intra-governmental activity on a quarterly basis.

Since EPA and OIG agree that the Agency is diligently working to reconcile intra-governmental transactions with our trading partners, we suggest replacing the first paragraph on pages 5 and 15 regarding *"EPA Should Continue Efforts to Reconcile Intra-governmental Transactions"* with the following text:

As of September 30, 2010, EPA reported $378 million in unresolved differences with 48 trading partners for intra-governmental transactions. Of that amount, $271 million was reported by Treasury to be material differences. The remaining $107 million represents amounts reported for nonverifying agencies, accruals, timing differences, and other agencies whose differences were not reported as material. According to the *Treasury Financial Manual*, verifying agencies are those that are required to report in the Government-wide Financial Report System. These include the 24 major Chief Financial Officer (CFO) Act agencies and 11 other agencies material to the *Financial Report of the United States Government*. Any agency not required is a non-verifying agency. Treasury policy requires verifying agencies to confirm and reconcile intra-governmental transactions with their trading partners with a goal of $0 net differences. Based on our review of correspondence with other agencies, EPA had difficulty eliminating these differences primarily because of differing accounting treatments and accrual methodologies among federal agencies, and because of a large reporting error made by one of EPA's trading partners. EPA's inability to eliminate its intragovernmental transactions contributes to a long-standing government-wide problem that hinders the ability of the U.S. Government Accountability Office to (GAO) render an opinion on the Consolidated Financial Statements of the Federal Government.

Additional comment for page 15: suggest replacing "un-reconciled differences" with "un-eliminated differences" since EPA has reconciled and knows basis for differences.

## 5 – EPA Improperly Closed Accounts When Cancelling Treasury Symbols

### Recommendations

We recommend the Chief Financial Officer:

11. Refund the cancelled funds to Treasury.

**Response: (Non-Concur)**

Subsequent to the issuance of the subject position paper, Office of Financial Management (OFM) found that the $933,299 advanced funds provided to the Working Capital Fund from the Environmental Program and Management (EPM) Fund (treasury symbol 682/30108) for services were improperly reflected as drawn down of an advance in treasury symbol 683/40108. The FY 2002/2003 funds were expended before cancelled, though the incorrect fund was referenced in this transaction. Therefore, there are no funds to be returned to Treasury. While we do not concur with the recommendation as written, we do acknowledge an error affected our reporting of customer advance funds and will make the appropriate adjusting entry to 683/40108 in FY 2011. We will also review our procedures and ensure processes for reconciliations are put in place so that no future issues occur.

12. Revise its cancellation procedures for the elimination of the balances from the cancelled treasury symbols.

**Response: (Concur)**

OFM will evaluate its procedures and revise them as necessary to ensure timely review of the balances in canceling treasury symbols. Appropriate procedures will be implemented in FY 2011.

13. Make appropriate adjustments to properly reflect balances.

**Response: (Concur)**

We will conduct analysis and provide guidance to ensure that balances are properly reported. Adjustments will be made during FY 2011 based on the results of our analysis.

**Responsible Managers**:

_____Signature/Date
Stefan Silzer, Acting Director, Office of Financial Manager, OCFO


_____Signature/Date
Raffael Stein, Director, Office of Financial Services


_____Signature/Date
Craig E. Hooks, Assistant Administrator, Office of Administration and Resources Management

# Distribution

Chief Financial Officer
Assistant Administrator for Administration and Resources Management
Assistant Administrator for Environmental Information and Chief Information Officer
General Counsel
Associate Administrator for Congressional and Intergovernmental Relations
Associate Administrator for External Affairs and Environmental Education
Director, Office of Policy and Resources Management, Office of Administration and
    Resources Management
Director, Office of Administration, Office of Administration and Resources Management
Director, Office of Technology Operations and Planning, Office of Environmental Information
Director, Office of Budget, Office of the Chief Financial Officer
Acting Director, Office of Financial Management, Office of the Chief Financial Officer
Director, Office of Financial Services, Office of the Chief Financial Officer
Director, Research Triangle Park Finance Center, Office of the Chief Financial Officer
Director, Cincinnati Finance Center, Office of the Chief Financial Officer
Director, Las Vegas Finance Center, Office of the Chief Financial Officer
Director, Office of Planning, Analysis, and Accountability, Office of the Chief Financial Officer
Director, Reporting and Analysis Staff, Office of the Chief Financial Officer
Director, Office of Technology Solutions, Office of the Chief Financial Officer
Director, Financial Policy and Planning Staff, Office of the Chief Financial Officer
Director, Accountability and Control Staff, Office of the Chief Financial Officer
Director, Payroll Management and Outreach Staff, Office of the Chief Financial Officer
Agency Audit Followup Coordinator
Agency Follow-up Official
Audit Followup Coordinator, Office of the Administrator
Audit Followup Coordinator, Office of the Chief Financial Officer
Audit Followup Coordinator, Office of Administration and Resources Management
Audit Followup Coordinator, Office of Solid Waste and Emergency Response
Audit Followup Coordinator, Office of Environmental Information
Audit Followup Coordinator, Office of Grants and Debarment, Office of Administration and
    Resources Management
Audit Followup Coordinator, Office of Financial Management, Office of the
    Chief Financial Officer
Audit Followup Coordinator, Office of and Financial Services, Office of the
    Chief Financial Officer

www.ingramcontent.com/pod-product-compliance
Lightning Source LLC
Chambersburg PA
CBHW081327310526
45789CB00018B/2473